DATE DUE

DEC 1 02

DEMCO 38-296

THE RISE AND FALL OF THE SOVIET EMPIRE

The Rise and Fall of the Soviet Empire

Raymond Pearson

St. Martin's Press
New York

St. Martin's Press, Scholarly and Reference Division,
175 Fifth Avenue, New York, N.Y. 10010

First published in the United States of America in 1998

This book is printed on paper suitable for recycling and
made from fully managed and sustained forest sources.

Printed in Hong Kong

ISBN 0–312–17405–5
ISBN 0–312–17407–1

Library of Congress Cataloging-in-Publication Data
Pearson, Raymond.
The rise and fall of the Soviet Empire / Raymond Pearson.
p.   cm. — (Studies in contemporary history)
Includes bibliographical references and index.
ISBN 0–312–17405–5 (cloth). — ISBN 0–312–17407–1 (paper)
1. Europe, Eastern—Politics and government—1945–1989.   2. Soviet
Union—Politics and government—1945–1991.   I. Title.   II. Series:
Studies in contemporary history (New York, N.Y.)
DJK50.P4 1997
947—dc21   96–52562
                                                       CIP

For Katy

CONTENTS

Contents

Series Editors' Preface

There are those, politicians among them, who feel that historians should not teach or write about contemporary events and people – many of whom are still living – because of the difficulty of treating such matters with historical perspective, that it is right to draw some distinction between the study of history and the study of current affairs. Proponents of this view seem to be unaware of the concept of contemporary history to which this series is devoted, that the history of the recent past can and should be written with a degree of objectivity. As memories of the Second World War recede, it is surely time to place in perspective the postwar history that has shaped all our lives, whether we were born in the 1940s or the 1970s.

Many countries – Britain, the United States and Germany among them – allow access to their public records under a thirty-year rule, opening up much of the postwar period to archival research. For more recent events, diaries, memoirs, and the investigations of newspapers and television, confirm the view of the famous historian Sir Lewis Namier that all secrets are in print provided you know where to look for them. Contemporary historians also have the opportunity, denied to historians of earlier periods, of interviewing participants in the events they are analysing. The problem facing the contemporary historian is, if anything, the embarrassment of riches.

In any case, the nature and extent of world changes since the late 1980s have clearly signalled the need for concise discussion of major themes in post-1945 history. For many of us the difficult thing to grasp is how dramatically the world has changed over recent years: the collapse of the Soviet Union and Russian communism; the end of Soviet hegemony over eastern Europe; the unification of Germany; the end of the Cold War; America's sense of a 'new world order'; the pace of integration in the European Community; the disintegration of Yugoslavia; the Middle East peace settlement; the continuing economic strength of Japan. Writing in a structured and cogent way about these seismic changes is what makes contemporary history so challenging, and we hope that the end result will convey some of this excitement and interest to our readers.

The general objective of this series, written entirely by members of the School of History, Philosophy and Politics of the University of Ulster, is to offer concise and up-to-date treatments of postwar themes considered of historical and political significance, and to stimulate critical thought about the theoretical assumptions and conceptual apparatus underlying interpretation of the topics under discussion. The series should bring some of the central themes and problems confronting students and teachers of recent history, politics and international affairs into sharper focus than the textbook writer alone could provide. The blend required to write contemporary history that is both readable and easily understood but also accurate and scholarly is not easy to achieve, but we hope that this series will prove worthwhile for both students and teachers interested in world affairs since 1945.

University of Ulster

T. G. Fraser
J. O. Springhall

CHRONOLOGY

1917	**Oct**	Bolshevik Revolution begins in Russia
1919–20		Paris Peace Settlement
1939	**Aug**	Nazi–Soviet Pact
	Sep	Start of Second World War
1939–41		Partition of eastern Europe between Nazi Germany and Soviet Union
1941	**Jun**	'Operation Barbarossa', German invasion of Soviet Union
1943		German Army defeated by Red Army at Stalingrad and Kursk
1943–4		Red Army reconquers German-occupied Soviet Union
1944–5		Red Army liberates most of eastern Europe
1945	**Feb**	Yalta Conference
	May	End of Second World War in Europe
	Jul–Aug	Potsdam Conference
1946	**Mar**	Churchill's 'Iron Curtain' speech
1947	**Mar**	Truman Doctrine
	Jun	Marshall Plan
	Oct	Cominform established

1948	**Feb**	Communist *coup* in Czechoslovakia
		Start of Stalin–Tito dispute
	Jun	Yugoslavia expelled from Cominform
		Berlin Blockade starts
1948–52		Anti-Titoist purges across eastern Europe
1949	**Jan**	Comecon established
	Apr	NATO established
	May	Berlin Blockade ends
1950–3		Korean War
1953	**Mar**	Death of Stalin
	Jun	Demonstrations in East Berlin suppressed
1955	**Feb**	Khrushchev replaces Malenkov as leader of Soviet Union
	May	Warsaw Pact established
		Soviet withdrawal from Austria
	Jun	Khrushchev–Tito declaration of reconciliation
1956	**Feb**	Khrushchev denounces Stalin in 'secret speech' at XX Congress of Communist party of Soviet Union
	Apr	Cominform disbanded
	Oct	'Polish October' headed by Gomulka
	Nov	Hungarian Uprising suppressed by Soviet Army
1957	**Jun**	Khrushchev purges opposition to his leadership
1961	**Aug**	Construction of Berlin Wall
	Oct	XXII Communist Congress initiates new de-Stalinisation
1962	**Oct**	Cuban missile crisis
1963	**Jul**	Plans for Comecon integration founder
1964	**Oct**	Khrushchev ousted by Kosygin and Brezhnev

1965	Mar	Ceausescu new leader of Romania
1968	Mar	Start of 'Prague Spring' headed by Dubcek
	Aug	Warsaw Pact invasion and occupation of Czechoslovakia
	Nov	'Brezhnev Doctrine' announced
1969–70		'Normalisation' imposed upon Czechoslovakia
1970	Dec	Gierek replaces Gomulka in Poland
1973		Global tripling of price of oil
1975	Aug	Helsinki Final Act
1977	Jan	Charter 77 founded in Czechoslovakia
	Oct	New 'Brezhnev Constitution' for Soviet Union
1978	Oct	Cardinal Wojtyla elected first Polish Pope
1979	Jun	Triumphal visit of Pope John Paul II to Poland
	Dec	Soviet invasion of Afghanistan
1980	Jul	Moscow Olympics boycotted by many states
	Aug	Solidarity emerges in Poland, led by Walesa
1981	Dec	Martial law in Poland imposed by Jaruzelski
1982	Nov	Death of Brezhnev, succeeded by Andropov
1983	Mar	Reagan announces US 'Star Wars' initiative
1984	Feb	Death of Andropov, succeeded by Chernenko
1985	Mar	Death of Chernenko, succeeded by Gorbachev
1986	Feb	XXVII Party Congress approves policy of *glasnost*
	Apr	Chernobyl nuclear accident
1987	Jan	Gorbachev authorises policy of *perestroika*
1988	Mar	Start of Soviet withdrawal from Afghanistan
	Aug	Strikes force Polish government to negotiate with Solidarity

1989	**May**	Hungary dismantles its Iron Curtain
	Jun	Solidarity landslide in Polish General Election
		Tiananmen Square massacre in China
	Jul	Gorbachev declaration of non-intervention in eastern Europe
	Aug	Solidarity-led government appointed in Poland
	Sep	Hungary permits exodus of East Germans to West
	Oct	Gorbachev speech in Helsinki seals 'Sinatra Doctrine'
	Nov	Breaching of Berlin Wall
		Fall of Zhivkov in Bulgaria
	Nov–Dec	'Velvet Revolution' in Czechoslovakia headed by Havel
	Dec	'Christmas Revolution' in Romania removes Ceausescu
1990	**Feb**	Communist party of Soviet Union renounces its monopoly status in new *demokratizatsia* policy
	Mar	Lithuania declares independence from Soviet Union
		Gorbachev elected executive President of Soviet Union
	May	Yeltsin elected Chairman of Russian Parliament
	Jul	'Summer of Sovereignty' across Soviet Union
	Oct	Germany formally reunified
1991	**Mar**	Referendum on future of Soviet Union
	Apr	Novo-Ogarev Accord on new federal treaty for Soviet Union
	Jun	Comecon formally dissolved
		Yeltsin elected President of Russia
	Jul	Warsaw Pact formally dissolved

Aug   Attempted *coup* in Moscow to stop new
            Union treaty
            Communist party discredited and dissolved

Dec   Ukraine declares independence from Soviet
            Union

            New Commonwealth of Independent States
            (CIS) agreed by Russia, Ukraine and Belarus

            Gorbachev resigns

            Soviet Union dissolved

GLOSSARY

apparat   the administrative 'apparatus' of the Soviet or Soviet-style state and establishment

apparatchik   a usually derogatory term for a Soviet civil servant or bureaucrat

Barbarossa   code name for the German invasion of the Soviet Union, 1941

Comecon   Council for Mutual Economic Assistance, 1949–91

Cominform   Communist Information Bureau, 1947–56

Comintern   (Third) Communist International, 1919–43

demokratizatsia   'democratisation', the official slogan of the Communist party of the Soviet Union after February 1990

glasnost   'openness', the official policy of free information and open government adopted by Gorbachev in January 1986

Gosplan   the economic 'State Planning Commission' of the Soviet Union

Gulag   official abbreviation of *Glavnoe Upravlenie Lagerei* (Chief Administration of Camps), the Soviet forced-exile system

intelligentsia   the educated élite, particularly those outside the establishment

korenizatsia   the 'indigenisation' of the Communist party, by which local (and especially non-Russian) personnel were recruited into the party to secure and wield local power

Kremlin   the symbolic, Moscow-sited locus of power and decision-making in the Soviet Union and Soviet Bloc

Neuordnung   the Nazi 'New Order' imposed (briefly and imperfectly) upon greater eastern Europe by military conquest after 1941

nomenklatura   the highest élite of the Soviet or Soviet-style personnel establishment

normalizatsia   'normalisation', the official Soviet euphemism for the repression of Czechoslovakia and the rest of the Soviet Empire after 1968

partiinost   'party-ness', prioritising the interests of the Communist party above all others, to the point of monopoly

perestroika   'transformation' or 'reconstruction', adopted by Gorbachev as the official slogan of the reforming Communist party of the Soviet Union in January 1987

Politburo   contraction of 'Political Bureau', the supreme executive 'cabinet' of the Soviet establishment before 1952 and after 1966 (and called the 'Presidium' 1952–66)

Pravda   'Truth', the official newspaper of the Communist party of the Soviet Union

samizdat   'self-publication' in manuscript by dissident writers refused publication by state censorship

sblizhenie   'getting closer', the official medium-term policy of encouraging the various nations and nationalities of the Soviet Union to 'draw together' under a broad Soviet allegiance and identity

Securitate   the 'Security' police of Romania under Ceausescu

sliyanie   'merging', the official long-term Soviet ambition for the 'fusion' of traditional national identities into a supranational Soviet identity

sputnik   'travelling companion', a Soviet artificial satellite, the first of which was launched in 1957

Stasi   'Staatsicherheit', the state security police of the German Democratic Republic

televorot   'TV revolution' transforming the attitudes of Soviet society over the late 1980s

Wehrmacht   'military power', the German Army under the Nazi regime

zastoi   'stagnation', the pejorative term adopted after 1987 to stigmatise the Brezhnev period from 1968 to 1983

Russia and Eastern Europe, 1992

1

YALTA 1945: LIBERATION OR OCCUPATION?

The year 1989 invites comparison with 1789 as a turning-point in modern European and world history. Accepted as a permanent fixture in an institutionalised 'Cold War' which had lasted over forty years, the Soviet Bloc fell sudden victim first to the decolonisation of its 'outer empire' of eastern Europe and then to the disintegration of its 'inner empire' of the Soviet Union over the cataclysmic years 1989–1991. The 'second 89', to employ a jubilant French headline, constituted an *annus mirabilis*, a miraculous year patently beyond the capacity of contemporaries, whether participants or bystanders, either to explain historically or comprehend politically. And yet, without contesting the unique dimensions of the extraordinary phenomenon of '1989', it is arguable almost to the point of being incontrovertible that the rise and fall of the Soviet Empire may only be understood fully as essentially the latest – but possibly the last – episode in a confrontation between nationalism and imperialism which has dominated eastern Europe for the last one hundred and fifty years.

The First World War and the Partition of Eastern Europe

Even before the dawning of the twentieth century, Europe was possessed by a sense of mounting confrontation between the irresistible force of oppositional nationalism and the immovable object of resident empire. To many contemporaries (and not a few modern historians), the late nineteenth century was above all the 'Age of Empire'. In western Europe, although something approximating to national states had been established over the early modern era, a competitive drive to global territorial expansion had recently created a Europocentric world in which lands and peoples in Africa and Asia were forcibly subordinated as overseas colonies within European-based international empires.

Across eastern Europe, three dynastic empires, in very different states of political health, embodied traditional power in an era of rising nationalist challenge. The Ottoman Empire, dubbed the 'Sick Man of Europe', was withdrawing spasmodically from territories in south-eastern Europe originally conquered in the sixteenth century, under the joint pressures of Balkan nationalist uprisings, rival imperial expansionism and Great Power concern to damp down the potentially explosive 'Eastern Question'. The Habsburg Empire, if not in the best of political health, was still considered chronically rather than mortally ill. Although the Empire was constrained to convert itself into the dual monarchy of Austria–Hungary in 1867, an expedient accommodation with Hungarian nationalist ambition, the effect of this *Ausgleich* ('compromise' or 'equalisation') was to stabilise the Habsburg domains against the mounting challenge of its extravagantly varied nationalities. The Russian Empire seemed in rudest political health where nationalist opposition was concerned, despite coming under increasing social and political pressures occasioned by rapid industrialisation and urbanisation. Perversely protected against the brunt of nationalism by its own social backwardness, the tsarist empire was sufficiently self-confident to mount an offensive against nationalism from the 1890s: a campaign of Russification was launched as a pre-emptive strike against minority nationalism immature enough to be vulnerable to tsarist suppression.

But although empire still commanded most of the pre-1914 global scene, the challenge from nationalism was demonstrably

2

mounting. While the later nineteenth century witnessed European colonisation of Africa and Asia, decolonisation from European empire had already featured in late eighteenth-century North America and early nineteenth-century South America. This ambiguous signal served to undermine the self-assurance of European imperialism and boost the self-confidence of European nationalism. A rash of new national states emerging in the Balkans (Greece in 1832, Serbia in 1833, Romania in 1856, Bulgaria in 1878 and Albania in 1912) demonstrated the burgeoning authority of nationalism, if admittedly at the expense of the manifestly weakest of the dynastic empires of eastern Europe. As the tide of nationalism washed north from the Balkans to surge into the Habsburg Empire and even lap at the littoral of the Russian Empire, nationalist expectations for the transformation of eastern Europe ran high.

Even so, despite the 'nationalist breakthrough' of German and Italian unification, which – together with Balkan liberation – has tempted historians to dub the late nineteenth century the 'Age of Nationalism', the victory of nationalism across eastern Europe was neither automatic nor inevitable. Once aroused, nationalist sentiment proved Teflon-clad against most imperial repression, lending nationalism an ineradicable defensive strength. But this did not mean that immediate and overwhelming nationalist victory was assured – or even intended. Many national groups appreciated the benefits of membership, however involuntary, of multinational empires, and therefore confined their ambition to greater autonomy rather than full independence. Even those nations committed to independence frequently found imperial power too strong to defeat: as the Poles, comprising the largest nation-without-a-state in Europe, had eventually to concede within the Russian Empire, the 'Balkan model' of national self-liberation was not necessarily applicable elsewhere in eastern Europe.

Approaching 1914, the global scenario was distinguished by neither 'Imperialism Triumphant' nor 'Nationalism Triumphant' but opportunistic ascendancies of imperialism and nationalism in different continents and regions. The sub-continent of eastern

Europe was itself subdivided between zones of nationalist ascendancy (in the ex-Ottoman Balkans), imperialist ascendancy (in the Russian Empire) and nationalist-imperialist stalemate (in the Habsburg Empire). In peacetime, imperial establishments were still robust enough to muster a respectable (and usually effective) rearguard action against nationalist challenge; while nationalist aspirations still lacked the resources and authority to claim a total or even widespread breakthrough against the resident imperial power systems.

What raised the *impasse* across eastern Europe, working so conspicuously to nationalist advantage and imperialist disadvantage, was the First World War. Paradoxically, the performance of the nationalist opposition over 1914–18 was not as good, and the performance of the imperial establishments was not as bad, as were either expected at the time or have been subsequently represented. Many contemporaries anticipated that the outbreak of war in 1914 would act as the detonator for an explosion of nationalist sentiment; but in practice nationalists failed to exploit the opportunities introduced by wartime until the last year of the war. By contrast, all three empires attracted a considerable solidarity of allegiance to their war efforts and performed unexpectedly well militarily, operating over a number of fronts in difficult circumstances through an unexpectedly prolonged period. All three empires of eastern Europe proved militarily too successful for their own political good in the First World War. If they had crumbled or surrendered earlier, they might well have survived in tolerable physical and political shape. By fighting on for years, they all suffered damage on a scale which practically guaranteed political revolution together with ultimate military defeat. Perversely, although the nationalists generally performed poorly and the empires acquitted themselves unexpectedly well, the cumulative impact of this unpredictably protracted war was to switch over the political ascendancy definitively from imperialism to nationalism.

Out of the unprecedented physical, human and psychological damage of the First World War emerged an almost desperate faith in a better future. Few could bring themselves to conclude that the unimaginable carnage of the internecine conflict which the Great Powers had entered so confidently – almost nonchalantly – in 1914, had been for nothing. Almost all believed (or at least affected to believe) that even a thundercloud of the magnitude of the First World War must have a silver lining. The sanguine political legacy of the war manifested itself in a differential boost to a variety of existing competing ideologies. The war had indisputably discredited and then fragmented the traditional dynastic empires of eastern Europe, but what political order was to replace them? The strained idealism generated by the war provided a fillip to constitutionalism, nationalism and socialism, with all three rival movements welcoming an upturn in their political fortunes. Nationalists and constitutionalists envisaged an evolutionary surge in their long-established authority, while socialists projected a revolutionary breakthrough in their previously disappointing prospects.

As a consequence, the most striking feature of interwar eastern Europe proved to be its geopolitical partition between an East legitimised by socialism and a West sanctioned by constitutionalism. But the indisputable appeal of insurgent nationalism forced an accommodation from both establishments. All the principal nations of eastern Europe had their right to sovereignty and self-determination enshrined in the international wave of constitution-making which was such a novel feature of the five years following the end of the First World War – effectively a breakthrough in the authority of nationalism. Just as the Western-licensed establishment of East–Central Europe was an expedient accommodation between nationalism and constitutionalism, so the Soviet-determined establishment further east was an expedient accommodation between nationalism and communism.

Interwar Soviet Europe

It was socialism, an optimistic ideology lent immeasurably strengthened authority by the First World War, which furnished the justification for the new Soviet establishment. Following the collapse of tsarism in March 1917 and the poor showing of its reluctant successor, the would-be democratic Provisional Government, the Bolsheviks under Vladimir Lenin and Leon Trotsky seized power in the Russian capital of Petrograd in October 1917. Among the Bolsheviks' articles of faith was the conviction that nationalism was a backward, anachronistic 'false dawn' whose influence would inevitably fade on exposure to the bright sun of socialism. But although avowedly socialist, the supremely pragmatic Bolshevik government appreciated that the long-lingering appeal of nationalism must be exploited and channelled rather than ignored or snubbed. To gain desperately needed support for the Bolsheviks, Lenin had promised 'national self- determination' to the minority nations of the Empire even before the fall of tsarism. For most of the civil war between the Russian 'Reds' and 'Whites' which dominated the years 1918–21, an official Bolshevik respect for nationalist obsession with escape from the 'prison of nations' prevailed for pragmatic and strategic reasons (Nahaylo and Swoboda, 1990).

Pointedly uninvited to participate in the Paris Peace Settlement by Western Allies who expected its ideologically obnoxious regime to collapse at any moment, Bolshevik Russia was too weak to prevent extensive decolonisation. Ex-tsarist properties to the west which secured and retained their independence during this period of Bolshevism's greatest danger included Finland, Estonia, Latvia, Lithuania and Poland. That Lenin's apparent magnanimity towards nationalist aspiration was dictated by expediency rather than ideology was, however, demonstrated by the ruthlessness with which less-advantaged nations to the east were forcibly 'returned to the socialist fold' when the opportunities presented themselves: Ukraine, Belorussia, Armenia, Georgia and Azerbaidzhan all had their attempts at independent statehood summarily guillotined by invasions of the Red Army over 1919–21 (McCauley, 1981).

Even so, the Bolshevik state which emerged shakily victorious after the debilitating civil war in 1921 recognised the wisdom of following a Leninist policy of restraint towards its non-Russian minorities, particularly those nationalities whose ambitions for independence had been so recently and brutally thwarted. Over 1922–4, the Bolshevik state was converted into the Soviet Union, ostensibly a constitutionally guaranteed multinational federation. Lenin's last political achievement, promulgated in the same week as his death in January 1924, was a Constitution which represented an expedient medium-term compromise between what was seen as the burgeoning authority of socialism and the declining but still formidable appeal of nationalism. In the complementary tactics of a constitutional 'national contract' with non-Russian nations and a mass-recruitment 'indigenisation' drive to induct non-Russians into the Communist party of the Soviet Union, Leninist strategy prevailed for the remainder of the 1920s (Nahaylo and Swoboda, 1990).

However, Leninist constitutionalism thereafter yielded to Stalinist authoritarianism. The right of secession for the union republics guaranteed by the Constitution of 1922–4 was never formally rescinded but the systematic centralisation of the Communist party under Josef Stalin removed the constitutional rights of non-Russians from the realm of practical politics. By the 'Second Revolution', begun in 1928, a deepening of the Leninist achievement through an expansion of state power over society propelled Soviet government towards totalitarianism. By 1936, Stalin could promulgate a new constitution which was hailed as the most democratic in the world but represented a cruel and surrealist travesty far removed from the increasingly grim realities of Soviet life. During the 1930s, all national groups were ruthlessly subordinated to centralised Communist party power, with the Ukrainians – the second largest nation after the Russians – mercilessly targeted for genocidal repression. Under Stalin, the Soviet Union became an entirely sham federation, in reality treating its non-Russian territories and nations as colonies within an authoritarian unitary jurisdiction which prompted uneasy memories of the pre-revolutionary Russifying tsarist empire (Nahaylo and Swoboda, 1990).

Even so, as a result of the loss of much of the western borderlands of Russia to independent nation-statehood over 1918–21, the Soviet Union was a lesser empire compared with its tsarist predecessor. Just how permanent the current jurisdiction of the Soviet Union might be was an issue with internal and especially external implications. In the leadership contest following Lenin's death in 1924, Stalin countered Trotsky's championship of 'permanent revolution' by espousing the prudent policy of 'Socialism in One Country'. Stalin readily conceded that to commit Soviet resources to the cause of the world revolution, as institutionally represented by the Third Communist International (or Comintern) established in 1919, possessed unimpeachable socialist legitimacy. He argued, however, that the current coincidence of undisguisable Soviet weakness and – doubtless temporary – capitalist strength rendered that commitment tactically inopportune for the 1920s (and incidentally threw the gravest doubts on Trotsky's political judgement). The alternative was to husband the still meagre resources of a Soviet Union battered by past military conflict, economic dislocation and social collapse to create a 'bastion of socialism'. At best, the Soviet Union would become the springboard for future world socialist revolution when capitalism underwent its next crisis. At worst, the Soviet Union would become an impregnable redoubt of socialism against an encircling capitalist world committed to interventionist *revanche*. With the defeat of Trotsky and the recognition of Stalin as Soviet leader in 1929, the concept of international revolution was played down and the defensive slogan of 'Socialism in One Country' became official dogma. The Soviet Union was effectively converted into a *status quo* power within Europe.

The 1930s paradoxically demonstrated both the past wisdom and future dispensability of 'Socialism in One Country' as the Soviet Union found itself fortuitously and uniquely advantaged by the Depression afflicting the West. Although never hermetically sealed from the outside world, the isolationist Soviet Union proved relatively insulated from the worst effects of capitalist Depression. The spectacle of capitalism in crisis was in itself a major boost to long-strained Soviet morale, in turn promoting a 'cult of personality' built upon Stalin's reputation for unique prescience. As capitalist Europe suffered economic collapse, social impoverishment, cultural dislocation and political polarisation, the prospects for recruitment to the Communist banner dramatically improved, raising the possibility of the early abandonment of the expedient 'Socialism in One Country' policy (McCauley, 1981). With recovery from the human and material damage inflicted by the combined First World War and Civil War now broadly complete within a new scenario of ongoing capitalist disarray, Stalin was increasingly tempted to re-employ socialist ideology (and Trotskyist strategy) to justify territorial expansionism to recover the 'lost territories' of the Soviet Union, should the opportunity present itself.

Interwar Versailles Europe

In the immediate aftermath of the First World War, the Western Allies had high hopes that the débâcle of 1914–18 would prove, to paraphrase another contemporary slogan, the 'War to Make the World Safe for Democracy'. Eastern Europe in particular was – rather patronisingly – perceived as a region economically, socially and culturally within hailing distance of the more sophisticated West. Released from the benighted political repression of dynastic empire, eastern Europe could now be expected to seize its chance to join the Western 'family of democratic nations'. Thanks to the war, Western democracy and constitutionalism had the opportunity, if not the certainty, of cultivating remoter parts of Europe hitherto beyond their power to reach. Eastern Europe should now be envisaged as an extended 'plantation of Western democracy', representing a definitive and irreversible breakthrough in the process by which Western democratic ideas spread out from their North Atlantic origins to colonise and eventually to liberate the entire wider world.

Within eastern Europe itself, however, it was less constitutionalism than nationalism which was seen as the beneficiary of the collapse of dynastic empire. If eastern Europe was indeed being colonised from outside, it was by a northward movement of southern nationalism rather than an eastward movement of western constitutionalism. The nineteenth-century record of the successful achievement of national statehood by indigenous movements in Greece, Serbia, Romania, Bulgaria and Albania within the shrinking Ottoman Empire could now be emulated by nations empowered by the wartime collapse of the Habsburg and Russian Empires. It was under the influence of this upsurge in nationalist ambitions and fortunes that President Woodrow Wilson of the USA proposed peace on the basis of 'Fourteen Points' in January 1918. This Allied blueprint for postwar Europe flashed a clear signal to nationalists that the Great Powers were recognising the refurbished authority of nationalism and, in particular, the necessity of replacing dynastic empires with authorised nation-states.

In this sanguine light, the victorious Allies effected the package of treaties that go under the traditional collective title of the Paris Peace Settlement, effectively an accommodation between Great Power grand strategy and indigenous east European nationalist ambition. In the hope that constitutionalism and nationalism could be the joint inspirations and legitimisers of democratic nation-states, the Allies made their recognition of each of the new states of East–Central Europe conditional upon their immediate adoption of Western-style constitutions. To bolster their geopolitical creation and favour the maintenance of constitutional government, the Allies provided financial aid which permitted a pleasing degree of economic progress and a tolerable level of democratic performance across the 'Versailles Europe' of the early and mid 1920s.

And yet, despite high early hopes for a constructive compact between nationalism and constitutionalism, the increasing destabilisation of 'Versailles Europe' over the later 1920s and 1930s owed much to the deficiencies of the Paris Peace Settlement. Each of the losing Central Powers in the First World War had been compelled to sign a politically humiliating and territorially punitive treaty of peace with the Western Allies: the Treaty of Versailles (June 1919) deprived Germany of significant tracts of territory to its east and west; the Treaty of St Germain (September 1919) reduced the defunct Habsburg Empire to a rump state of Austria; the Treaty of Neuilly (November 1919) more than cancelled all the wartime territorial conquests made by Bulgaria; the Treaty of Trianon (June 1920) reduced the newly independent Hungary to one-third of the size of the former 'Kingdom of Hungary'; and the Treaty of Sèvres (August 1920) licensed Allied acquisitions so substantial as to damage and discredit the Ottoman Empire irremediably (Pearson, 1994).

The geopolitical impact of the Paris Peace Settlement was to create a 'Versailles Europe' conspicuously (and fatally) divided between winners and losers. The common denominator of the 'victims of Versailles' – Germany, Austria, Bulgaria, Hungary and Ottoman Turkey – was to have fought on the losing side in the First World War. The common denominator of the 'beneficiaries of Versailles' – Poland, Romania, Czechoslovakia and the Kingdom of the Serbs, Croats and Slovenes (thankfully renamed Yugoslavia in 1929) – was to have fought for or demonstrated a clear commitment to the winning side in the First World War. For a geopolitical settlement supposedly based upon the principle of national self-determination, the Paris Peace treaties were demonstrably unjust: cavalierly redistributing territory that was not theirs to give, in a triumphalist fashion based upon Great Power favouritism and grand strategy, the Allies shamelessly stripped the assets of the 'victims' in order to endow the 'beneficiaries' with more territory than they 'deserved'.

The geopolitical result of the First World War was therefore not only an eastern Europe partitioned between the Soviet Union and the 'successor states' but a 'Versailles Europe' so fatally flawed that it was only a matter of time before it was successfully challenged. No settlement which so humiliatingly penalised Germany and so severely disadvantaged the Soviet Union could seriously be expected to last. Once the two powers destined to dominate twentieth-century Europe, temporarily weakened by war over 1914–20, achieved material and morale recovery in the mid-1930s, 'Versailles Europe', and especially independent eastern Europe, was doomed.

'Versailles Europe' found itself challenged on every front. Economically, the break-up of the dynastic empires posed

formidable problems of readjustment. The successor states only –
and belatedly – appreciated the taken-for-granted economic
benefits of integration within the large-scale Austro-Hungarian
Empire once it had disappeared. Even during the relatively
prosperous 1920s, the eastern European states could only survive
financially through Western investment: for example, in 1928
some 60 per cent of Polish capital was foreign. In the 1930s, the
impact of the world Depression was bound to be severe on an
area which combined only modest modernisation with over-
reliance on external investment.

Political problems proved irresolvable. So divisive was the
Paris Peace Settlement that no solidarity even of protective self-
interest against the looming threat from Germany to the west
and the Soviet Union to the east ever overcame the mutual
hostility which poisoned relations between the eastern European
states. For all its publicity of principle, the Peace Settlement
conspicuously failed to deliver on its objective of converting
eastern Europe from empires to nation-states. None of the new
states authorised over 1919–20 was actually a nation-state, simultaneously including all co-nationals and excluding all non-
nationals. The state closest to ethnic homogeneity was Hungary,
whose population was some 85 per cent Hungarian only through
being compelled by the Treaty of Trianon to surrender two-
thirds of its previous territory, and at the cost of seeing one-
third of all Hungarians now marooned in neighbouring states.
While the victims of Versailles were forced closer to nation-
statehood only by territorial reduction, the beneficiaries of Versailles were expanded into mini-empires by a combination of
nationalist land-grabbing and Great Power concern to prevent
a Balkanisation which would leave eastern Europe vulnerable
to Soviet advance. The conflict-model precipitated by the
Paris Settlement was accentuated by bitter squabbles over long-
running minority issues which peaked in the later 1930s
(Pearson, 1983).

The 1930s were also notable for the effective withdrawal of the
West from eastern Europe. As already remarked, the economies
of the eastern European states were so fragile that Western

patronage was vital to their well-being over the 1920s and 1930s. The reliance on foreign 'subsidisation' which was merely regrettable in the 1920s became patently disastrous in the 1930s. As the repercussions of the Wall Street Crash washed over western Europe, the Great Powers of the USA, France and Great Britain were constrained to concentrate their resources on the welfare of their own populations, necessarily at the cost of traditional investment in eastern Europe (Okey, 1986). As financial disaster struck across 'Versailles Europe', societies which had been spoilt by past patronage reacted bitterly to what they regarded as their desertion or even betrayal by the wealthy West (Crampton, 1994).

Though less dramatic, political withdrawal by the West was also self-evident. Eastern Europe proved a grievous disappointment to Western liberals hoping for a permanent conversion to constitutionalism. Democratic institutional transplants inserted by Western intrusive surgery were typically rejected as alien to the eastern European body politic. Virtually all the states of eastern Europe abandoned implanted democracy in favour of right-wing authoritarianism, with Hungary in 1920, Poland in 1926 and Yugoslavia in 1929 as the earlier and perhaps most dispiriting examples (Polonsky, 1975). Although this trend to authoritarianism over constitutionalism was continent-wide, mirroring the Fascist revolution in Italy from 1922, the Stalinist 'Second Revolution' in the Soviet Union from 1928 and the Nazi revolution in Germany from 1933, the disappointment in the West at the cumulative collapse of eastern European democracy was keenly felt. By the time that the Depression forced the economic abandonment of eastern Europe in the early 1930s, the West's political faith in, and commitment to, an eastern Europe which was 'flunking democracy' had been irreversibly undermined (Roskin, 1994: 26).

The final, and crucial, dimension of Western withdrawal was military and strategic. International regulation of disputes lost all credibility with the embarrassing and repeated failures of intervention and sanction by the League of Nations in the 1930s. As the victims of Versailles drifted into the revisionist camp of

Germany and Italy, the beneficiaries of Versailles relied ever more completely and desperately on the West for the military maintenance of 'Versailles Europe'. Yet with the long-established withdrawal of the USA from Europe increasingly echoed by the faltering commitment of France and especially Great Britain to eastern Europe, a power vacuum opened up in the course of the 1930s, which became irresistible to the principal anti-Versailles power of Germany and tempting to the principal non-Versailles power of the Soviet Union (Simons, 1993).

The test-case for independent eastern Europe was played out over Czechoslovakia in 1938 (Seton-Watson, 1945: 394). In economic, social and political terms, Czechoslovakia was indisputably the prime performer of interwar eastern Europe. As the most western of the eastern European states, Czechoslovakia was the only state to retain a constitutional system by the late 1930s (Polonsky, 1975). Although this does not necessarily mean that Czechoslovakia's democratic credentials were impeccable – the treatment of non-Czechs within what Slovaks in particular condemned as a 'Czech Empire' was too problematic for such an unqualified endorsement – there is no doubt that, in eastern European terms, Czechoslovakia was constitutionally the best of a bad batch (Schopflin, 1993).

Czechoslovakia's reputation as the darling of the West made her abandonment by Britain and France, in the face of German threats at Munich in September 1938, all the more shocking for eastern Europe. Nazi Germany, which had already incorporated Austria by the *Anschluss* of March 1938 in defiance of both the Versailles and St Germain treaties of 1919, occupied the German-speaking Sudetenland region of Czechoslovakia in September 1938 and subsequently the entire Czech-speaking portion of the partitioned state of Czechoslovakia in March 1939. Eastern Europe was left with no remaining illusions about its past or future. Regarding the past, Munich demonstrated that interwar eastern Europe had never been truly independent. Western economic, political and military support had sustained at best a 'dependent independence' for eastern Europe; at worst, the pseudo-independence of eastern Europe had been no more than a calculated (or even unknowing) bluff, finally called by Adolf Hitler with devastating effect in September 1938. Regarding the future, 'Munich 1938' represented, directly or indirectly, the imminent guillotining of eastern Europe's hopes for 'Versailles Europe'. If Czechoslovakia was indeed, in the British Prime Minister Neville Chamberlain's famously dismissive phrase, 'a far-off country of which we know little' to the Western powers, then the remainder of eastern Europe could expect no support from the West and no mercy from Nazi Germany (Taylor, 1961).

The Second World War and the Repartition of Eastern Europe

The lesser surprise of 1939 was the outbreak of what became the Second World War. Although the lesson of Munich was ostensibly that the West had abandoned eastern Europe to German depredations, the subsequent liquidation and partition of Czechoslovakia converted Europe to a reluctant recognition of the probability, if not the inevitability, of Great Power conflict. Rightly interpreting Munich as his greatest diplomatic triumph, Hitler drew the false conclusion that the Western 'appeasers' had tacitly granted Germany *carte blanche* for the takeover of the remainder of eastern Europe. Although the presence of a substantial German minority in the 'Polish Corridor' gave Hitler a more convincing case for German expansionism against Poland in late 1939 than against what remained of Czechoslovakia in early 1939, the stance of the Western powers had now switched from pragmatic appeasement to reluctant confrontation (Taylor, 1961). Hitler's diplomatic miscalculation that, despite the Franco-British guarantee to Poland in late March 1939, his raid on Poland would be accepted as complaisantly in the West as his raid on Czechoslovakia precipitated war in September 1939 between Germany, Britain and France.

The bigger surprise of 1939 was that Poland was invaded by, and subsequently partitioned between, Germany and the Soviet Union working in concert. Meetings between the German foreign minister Joachim von Ribbentrop and the Soviet foreign commissar Vyacheslav Molotov in August 1939 produced secret protocols confirming joint and cooperative action by the *Wehrmacht* and Red Army for the conquest of independent Poland and the division of its territory (Tolstoy, 1981; Crampton, 1994). Geographically located between Germany and Russia but historically not up to the geopolitical weight of its powerful neighbours, Poland suffered the not-unfamiliar fate of a 'Fifth Partition' in September 1939.

The East–West partition of Poland was not, however, merely a one-off deal to subordinate the largest of the east European states, a twentieth-century equivalent of the tripartite Great Power partitions of Poland in 1774, 1793, 1795 and 1815. 'Warsaw 1939' turned out to be only the first instalment in a grand strategy to obliterate all the independent states of eastern Europe and convert them into dependent colonies of an expanded Germany and a greater Soviet Union. In the course of the next eighteen months, Hitler and Stalin partitioned eastern Europe between themselves. Germany directly annexed western Poland, the Bohemian and Moravian provinces of Czechoslovakia and the Slovenian region of Yugoslavia, whilst retaining Slovakia, Bulgaria, an enlarged Hungary and a reduced Romania as increasingly dependent client states. The Soviet Union annexed eastern Poland, eastern Finland and the Bessarabian region of northern Romania, and incorporated Estonia, Latvia and Lithuania 'by invitation' in June 1940 (Tolstoy, 1981). To the despairing peoples of the east, the Nazi–Soviet pacts of August and September 1939 comprised a twentieth-century version of the 1807 Treaty of Tilsit, by which Bonaparte and Alexander I agreed to divide Europe into Napoleonic and tsarist spheres of influence.

Stalin's reasons for striking such a grandiose but controversial geopolitical deal with Hitler have never been definitively determined. The line of traditional Soviet historiography was that all-seeing Stalin appreciated the implacable hostility of Nazism to Communism but, recognising the military unpreparedness of the peace-loving Red Army relative to the demonic efficiency of the

Wehrmacht, employed his uniquely Machiavellian skills to win a precious breathing-space to enable the Soviet Union to withstand the inevitable German onslaught (Tolstoy, 1981). For the West to condemn the Nazi–Soviet Pact was purest humbug: it was Western appeasement of Hitler in 1938 that necessitated and legitimised Eastern 'appeasement' of Hitler in 1939. The apparently shameful compact between the Soviet Union and Nazi Germany had therefore to be viewed as an adroitly executed and militarily indispensable delaying ploy without which the Soviet people would not have survived capitalist invasion.

An alternative interpretation argues that Stalin was attempting (and believed he had secured) a permanent carve-up of eastern Europe guaranteed by joint Soviet–German self-interest. From the very instant of the October *coup* of 1917, Lenin had expected the Russian example to inspire Communist revolution throughout Europe. Given the failure of spontaneous inspiration, the creation of the Comintern in 1919 gave notice that the Soviet-backed subversion of the wider capitalist world – and especially vulnerable 'Versailles Eastern Europe' – would assume a high priority for the Soviet Union (Crampton, 1994). And yet, by the early 1930s, the embarrassing failure of the Comintern to deliver a single victory for socialism forced Stalin into either accepting the capitalist *status quo* outside the 'Bastion of Socialism' or adopting an opportunism born of desperation. The Munich Crisis of 1938 persuaded Stalin to switch abruptly from the defensive former option articulated by Maxim Litvinov to the expansionist latter option associated with Vyacheslav Molotov, moving in the course of 1939 to seal an equitable and permanent division of the spoils of eastern Europe between the Soviet Union and Germany.

Whatever the precise planning of Stalin, the effect of the accord between Germany and the Soviet Union for the period from August 1939 to June 1941 was grim. Watched by a helpless West, Hitler and Stalin collaborated in the dismemberment of East–Central Europe, gradually advancing their respective jurisdictions at the expense of a dwindling middle zone, until their spheres of influence abutted to effect the complete East–West partition of 'Versailles Eastern Europe'.

Operation Barbarossa

The second phase in eastern Europe's ordeal in the Second World War was Hitler's attempt, imperfectly realised, to construct a continental *Neuordnung* or Nazi 'New Order' which necessitated the disruption of the 'twentieth-century Tilsit'. Hitler had never seen the pact with Stalin as anything but an expedient deal geared to the politico-military demands of 1939 – and 1940 brought changes so momentous that Hitler made the fateful (and, as it turned out, fatal) decision to turn on his erstwhile partner.

Two military episodes combined to prompt a revolution in Hitler's grand strategy. In the course of 1940, a 'phoney war' in which Germany, Britain and France seemed reluctant to draw blood was succeeded by an all-too-real western campaign of *Blitzkrieg* by which Germany successfully overran Holland, Belgium, Denmark, Norway and, most spectacularly, France over the three months of April to June. Such a stunning triumph for the *Wehrmacht*, within a time-frame beyond the wildest dreams of the Nazi leadership, convinced Hitler of the invincibility of German arms.

Over the same period, incontrovertible evidence of the relative weakness of the Red Army was becoming available to German military intelligence. Persistent rumours of a wide-ranging Stalinist purge of the Russian Army high command and officer corps over 1938 were dramatically corroborated by the poor performance of the Red Army against Finland in the so-called 'Winter War' of 1939–40. Although Stalin eventually secured the east Finnish territory over which the war was fought, the casualties on the Soviet side were horrendous. The historical inference was obvious: Stalin's prime motivation for accord with Germany in late 1939 had been less territorial greed than military fear of facing a *Wehrmacht* onslaught alone with a temporarily sub-standard army. The strategic lesson of the Winter War was equally stark: if the Red Army experienced such difficulties defeating the mini-power of Finland, then its prospects against a Great Power army were bleak (Tolstoy, 1981).

Proof of both German military might and Soviet military weakness over 1940 persuaded Hitler to abandon his strategy of partition in favour of total power. German intelligence reports suggested that the Red Army was recovering from the self-inflicted wound of the Stalinist purge and therefore the gap between German and Russian military capability was already closing. The recommendation was accordingly that if the *Führer* was considering war with the Soviet Union (as threatened since the writing of *Mein Kampf* in 1923), strategic considerations dictated that the sooner the war was undertaken the better (Tolstoy, 1981). By now convinced that Stalin's readiness to collaborate since 1938 was based on military weakness and political bluff, Hitler decided in November 1940 to invade the Soviet Union. There would never be a better chance to liquidate Russian Communism.

Approved by Hitler in December 1940 to commence in mid-May 1941, 'Operation Barbarossa' was actually launched on 22 June 1941, deferred some six weeks by a *Wehrmacht* campaign to subdue recalcitrant Yugoslavia, effectively the last remnant of 'Versailles Eastern Europe'. Despite the delay, the initial German attack on the Soviet Union, the biggest military action in history at the time, appeared stunningly successful (McCauley, 1981). Much of the responsibility both for the invasion itself and its early success must lie with Stalin. It was Stalin who had neurotically purged his own army just when it was needed at peak performance, thereby tempting, indeed virtually inviting Hitler to attack. It was Stalin who ignored warnings of invasion from both the West and his own intelligence services, then went into paralysed shock for a month when the invasion came. It was Stalin who had purged and repressed the Ukrainians and Belorussians so murderously in the 1930s that they could not conceive of a fate worse than Stalinist rule and therefore welcomed the advancing *Wehrmacht* as liberators in 1941 and were prepared to collaborate *en masse* with the German occupation authorities of the *Neuordnung*.

No empire can be maintained by military conquest alone, and the *Neuordnung* initially (and entirely sensibly) set out to exploit the national divisions of eastern Europe to concoct a deliberately counter-Versailles German-dominated establishment. Following the Napoleonic precept of favouring the nations penalised by the *ancien régime*, Hitler consciously demoted the victors of Versailles and promoted the victims of Versailles: the Poles, Czechs and Serbs were ignominiously deprived of statehood; the Hungarians and Bulgarians recovered territory lost in 1919–20; and the Slovaks and Croats were granted unprecedented (though still limited) self-determination following the German liquidation of (respectively) Czechoslovakia and Yugoslavia. Within newly conquered Soviet territory, an *Ostministerium* ('Ministry for the East') under Isaac Rosenberg promised greater autonomy for the Ukraine and Belorussia within the *Neuordnung* than had ever existed under the tsarist, Leninist and especially Stalinist regimes (Pearson, 1983). Headed by Nazi-licensed 'quislings', nations favoured by the *Neuordnung* were of course required to express their gratitude in the most practical manner (under the ever-present threat of the summary withdrawal of their recently granted privileges).

However, the political strategy of the *Neuordnung* was quickly subordinated to more insistent military and ideological priorities. The German war-machine exploited the resources and manpower of its conquered peoples increasingly ruthlessly, with little discrimination between the nominally 'favoured' and 'penalised' nations; while the racist Nazi belief in Aryan superiority bred a contemptuous maltreatment of all *Untermenschen* ('sub-humans') across eastern Europe. Non-German nations and nationalities soon became united in a consensus of alienation from the *Neuordnung*. For instance, Ukrainians who initially welcomed German 'liberation' in summer 1941, volunteered to join the specifically Ukrainian 'Nightingale' and 'Roland' divisions raised within the *Wehrmacht* and were prepared to serve Germany as *Ostarbeiteren* ('Workers from the East'), were subsequently repelled by brutal and repressive German treatment, notably the massacres at Babi Yar near Kiev, which claimed 90 000 Jewish and 50 000 Ukrainian lives in December 1941. Increasingly driven by fanatical ideological and desperate military preoccupations, the Nazi leadership often almost gratuitously antagonised all the nations of eastern Europe, wantonly wasting the opportunity to inject political stabilisation into the *Neuordnung*.

The End of the Nazi 'New Order'

Ultimately, of course, the success or permanence of the *Neuordnung* was dependent on German military performance rather than political strategy. With all the smugness of hindsight, it seems self-evident that Hitler's expansionist ambition outran German military capability (Kennedy, 1988). From the very start of the invasion of Russia, German plans went ominously wrong. The six-week delay in launching 'Operation Barbarossa', which later enabled the Yugoslavs to claim that they had unselfishly (if inadvertently) saved the Soviet Union from extinction, prevented the *Wehrmacht* from achieving its objective of the capture of all three leading cities of the Soviet Union: by the time that the Russian climate brought the campaign season of 1941 to a close, the Germans had taken Kiev but neither Leningrad nor Moscow. The early and bitter winter of 1941–2, for which the *Wehrmacht* was inadequately prepared, introduced a year-long stalemate infinitely more advantageous to the Russian than the German war effort. From the winter of 1942–3 began a slow but accelerating and eventually inexorable counter-offensive by the Red Army: by defeating the Germans at Stalingrad in January 1943, the Russians delivered a stunning psychological blow to the previously undefeated *Wehrmacht*; by the defeat at Kursk in July 1943, the Red Army decisively broke the German armies on the Eastern Front. Over 1943–4, the Red Army liberated (or re-occupied) all the German-conquered territory of the Soviet Union (McCauley, 1981). Over 1944–5, the Red Army crossed the Soviet frontier to pursue the retreating

Wehrmacht across an eastern Europe which had never before experienced Soviet authority.

Just what the Red Army's advance through most of eastern Europe might mean politically dominated a conference between Franklin Roosevelt of the USA, Winston Churchill of the United Kingdom and Josef Stalin of the Soviet Union, meeting at the tsarist palace of Livadia, near the Crimean resort of Yalta, in February 1945. In one sense, the Yalta Conference was inexcusably late: there had been no meeting of the 'Big Three' to coordinate political responses to the fast-changing military situation for the fourteen months since the Teheran Conference of November–December 1943 (Ionescu, 1965). In another sense, the conference was impractically premature: three months before victory in Europe (and six months before victory in Asia), the Big Three were attempting to second-guess the shape of peacetime Europe well before the fighting was over. The prospect for eastern Europe was accordingly subject to the wildest speculation, conspicuously unresolved by the Delphic official pronouncements of the Yalta Conference (Young, 1991). Was eastern Europe being liberated or occupied? With the *Neuordnung* patently on the eve of liquidation, would its replacement be a restored 'Versailles Europe', as the Allied joint 'Declaration on Liberated Europe' seemed to suggest? Or the 'Greater Soviet Union' within a repartitioned European continent feared by so many east Europeans? (Stokes, 1991) 'Yalta 1945' epitomised the contradictions of interwar dependent independence and the vagaries of wartime geopolitics without establishing any certainties for post-Second World War eastern Europe.

2

BELGRADE 1948: COLD WAR EMPIRE

Both the fortuitous ambiguities and deliberate ambivalencies of the Yalta Conference in February 1945 were definitively resolved over the following five years. The interwar and wartime eastward shift of the locus of continental authority over eastern Europe from Paris to Munich, then from Warsaw to Yalta, irresistibly placed the ultimate postwar fate of eastern Europe at the disposal of Stalin's Soviet Union. There were to be four sequential phases in the creation of a 'Soviet Empire' in the course of the later 1940s, each phase a response to a different stimulus, each phase overlaying its predecessor to effect a cumulative and composite Stalinist imperial establishment.

Military Occupation

Over 1944–5, most of German-occupied eastern Europe was emancipated by the advance of the Red Army. The pincer-movement invasion of central Europe from east and west had been authorised jointly by Churchill, Roosevelt and Stalin at Teheran in November–December 1943 (Ionescu, 1965). The Red Army occupation of eastern Europe was therefore a necessary and yet incidental product of the Allied military victory over Nazi Germany, sanctioned in advance by the West.

The permanence or otherwise of that military occupation was considered long before the final defeat of Nazi Germany and came to dominate the Great Power agenda during 1945. The ideal scenario for the Western powers was the peacetime withdrawal of the intervening armies as soon as was practicable after the end of the war to permit an early restitution of prewar 'Versailles Europe'. After all, Britain and France had declared war over the German invasion of Poland in September 1939. Following the defence of 'Versailles Poland', what else had the Second World War been fought for but the overthrow of the Nazi *Neuordnung* and the restoration of pre-1939 Versailles Europe?

Such an optimistic Western scenario evaporated over the last year of the war. As early as July 1944, the Soviet Union established the Lublin Committee as its favoured agency in Poland, an unmistakable indication of Soviet insistence on a political (and very possibly a permanent) stake in Polish affairs. Soviet intentions were confirmed by formal recognition of a Lublin Committee-based provisional government of Poland announced in December 1944 (McCauley, 1981). On a broader geopolitical scale, in October 1944, Churchill and Stalin drew up the so-called 'Percentage Agreements' which laid down the relative degrees of influence for the United Kingdom and the Soviet Union in the countries of the postwar Balkans. At the Yalta Conference in February 1945, the implicit handover to an already expanded 1940-style Soviet Union of most of eastern Europe was agreed, with modest conditions and token safeguards, by all three Great Powers (Roskin, 1994). By the time of the Potsdam Conference after final victory in Europe in July–August 1945, the Western abandonment of eastern Europe was explicit.

The explanation for the complaisance of the West regarding eastern Europe is not elusive. Especially in the climate of Allied collaboration against Germany in a war which was still not won, no military challenge to the Red Army was feasible in an area so manifestly outside the traditional Western field of operations (Dunbabin, 1994). As at Munich in 1938, the West bowed to *force majeure,* abandoning eastern Europe to whomsoever was powerful enough to claim it. The 'Percentage Agreements' of late 1944 continued the Western appeasement policy of 1938: Churchill was appeasing Stalin in 1944 in much the same spirit that Chamberlain had appeased Hitler in 1938. Churchill's action has naturally excited considerable controversy. To critics, such early Western defeatism, which started with a broad hint from Churchill at Teheran that Stalin was entitled to Poland, represented an attitude of craven surrender which was not only morally reprehensible but irresponsibly encouraged the aggressor to demand more (Stokes, 1991). To supporters, the agreements were a pragmatic response calculated to avoid gratuitously provoking the aggressor, enabling the West to retain at least some say in the fate of eastern Europe (Ionescu, 1965). The Second World War had replaced Germany with the Soviet Union as the natural dominator of eastern Europe, and the West had little realistic option but to defer to Soviet demands in 1945.

The geopolitical linkage between the European and Pacific theatres of the Second World War also contributed towards delivering eastern Europe into Soviet hands. At the time of the Yalta Conference, Allied military victory in Europe was assured and imminent. The same could not be said of Allied victory in Asia. With American forces experiencing continuing difficulties defeating the Japanese in the Philippines and later Okinawa, Roosevelt wished to preserve the option of Soviet military intervention in the Far East, which would certainly not be furthered by alienating Stalin. Tacit American acquiescence over Soviet penetration and control of eastern Europe was a diplomatic quid pro quo, even a Western bribe, to engage essential Soviet military help in the protracted war against Japan.

By the time of the Potsdam Conference, the availability of the atomic bomb was transforming American strategy; but too late to save eastern Europe from a Soviet takeover. The atomic bomb was employed at Hiroshima and Nagasaki to minimise American casualties and force an early Japanese surrender – but also to warn the Soviet Union against transferring its expansionist ambitions from Europe to Asia. Harry Truman's intimidatory tactic secured its desired effect of Soviet containment in Asia, but at the price of accepting the geopolitical *fait accompli* of Soviet territorial takeover of militarily occupied eastern Europe. For a complex of military, diplomatic and political reasons, the endgame of the Second World War saw the West powerless to restore interwar 'Versailles Europe'.

Economic Exploitation

All too often, evaluation of the parameters of Western strategy implicitly presupposes that the Soviet Union always planned to maintain a military (and subsequently a political) presence in eastern Europe, ignoring or neglecting the fundamental question of why Stalin should wish to retain Red Army-occupied eastern Europe once the war was over.

The supreme internal stimulus for Stalinist expansionism was the desperate physical plight of the Soviet Union resulting from its Pyrrhic victory in the Second World War. The damage inflicted upon the European Soviet Union by war over the period 1941–4 is almost impossible to exaggerate. Although Stalin was to claim that the Soviet death toll was (only!) 10 million, Western experts calculated that 20 million was nearer the mark. Secret official statistics released under *glasnost* now indicate that the actual figure was 8.6 million military dead and around 18 million civilian dead, producing the astronomical total of almost 27 million killed. To the dead must be added the permanently handicapped and incapacitated, with conservative estimates putting the injured military total at 22 million. Demographic damage, always the most difficult for any society to recover from, was heavier for the Soviet Union, in both absolute and relative terms, than for any other combatant state in the Second World War (Kennedy, 1988).

The economic damage visited upon European Russia was also cataclysmic in scale. Most of Soviet industry was located in the European rather than the Asian Soviet Union and was extensively damaged in the war zone over 1941–4. As the *Wehrmacht* advanced in 1941, the retreating Red Army adopted a 'scorched earth' policy of destroying industry: better to liquidate valuable resources than to allow them to fall into the hands of the enemy. From 1942 to 1943, a high proportion of surviving industry was destroyed by war damage and what remained was over-exploited by both the German and Soviet military authorities. And as the Red Army advanced in 1944, the retreating *Wehrmacht* destroyed what little industry remained in their own 'scorched earth' policy. For matching reasons, and even more crucially in the short term, agriculture suffered similar catastrophic damage. As a cruel final irony, Russia experienced its worst drought of the twentieth century in 1946, causing failed harvests in both 1946 and 1947. As if the Soviet Union had not suffered enough during the war, the first years of peacetime brought the Soviet people, already enduring a disastrous housing shortage, to the very brink of mass starvation (McCauley, 1981).

The resources available to the Soviet Union to stage a recovery from the Second World War were limited. External sources of investment, funding or aid proved unavailable. The foreign investment which had fuelled industrialisation in the late tsarist period was not forthcoming for a socialist state whose initial actions in October 1917 had included the sequestration of foreign property and the repudiation without compensation of all foreign debt. The exceptional Allied wartime aid which had materially assisted the Soviet military advance during 1943–5 was not to continue after the end of the war: the USA stopped wartime Lend-Lease in May 1945 and a desperate Soviet application for a six-billion-dollar loan was pointedly 'mislaid' in 1946 (Dunbabin, 1994).

If the internal resources of the Soviet Union were extensively damaged and external resources proved unforthcoming, Stalin had little option but to exploit what resources had become recently available to him through military eventuality. Emancipated eastern Europe had suffered from war more differentially than the European Soviet Union. Some parts of eastern Europe, notably Poland and Serbia, had certainly been amongst the most severely damaged (Simons, 1993). Other parts, like Bohemia and Bulgaria, had survived relatively unscathed. But few areas of eastern Europe had suffered damage to equal or surpass that of the European Soviet Union: eastern Europe as a whole was in better, or at least less bad, shape than the Soviet Union.

The desperate Soviet economic position at the end of the Second World War made a strategy of exploitation of eastern Europe backed by the occupying forces of the Red Army virtually irresistible. What may be termed a 'plunder policy' was unceremoniously adopted. At first, with no certainty of remaining in eastern Europe for any extended period, Soviet authority followed a 'smash and grab' tactic, physically transporting and relocating east European industrial assets within the Soviet Union (Dunbabin, 1994). But as the logistical difficulties of such a laborious transfer become apparent, Soviet strategy switched to systematic extortion premised on a permanent or semi-permanent Soviet tenure of eastern Europe. The exigencies of Soviet economic recovery necessarily undermined any early prospect of Soviet withdrawal and determined an increasingly extended time-scale for the Soviet presence in eastern Europe.

The moral justification for this Soviet plunder policy was threefold. First, the Soviet Union was exacting financial reimbursement from the defeated enemy on the time-hallowed principle, 'to the victor the spoils', updated by the precedent of the Allied insistence on reparations from the Central Powers after the First World War. Secondly, the Soviet Union expanded the accusation of 'war guilt' beyond Germany. With some eastern European states (like Hungary) choosing to ally with peacetime Nazi Germany and more (like Slovakia) prepared to collaborate with the wartime *Neuordnung*, the Soviet Union felt entitled to visit selective punishment on the guilty and demand literally punitive reparations (a principle accepted by the Western powers). Thirdly and more broadly, the 'innocence' or 'guilt' of eastern Europe was peripheral to the ultimate cause of the recovery of the Soviet Union. All other considerations and all other states had to be subordinated to the supreme Soviet priority. 'Innocent' states would pay plenty and 'guilty' states would pay more; but all states within the military jurisdiction of the Kremlin would be required to contribute lavishly. The 'bastion of socialism', beleaguered since 1917 and unprecedentedly damaged since 1941, was entitled to adopt any and all means to ensure its survival in a relentlessly hostile capitalist world.

The systematic economic exploitation phase followed and overlaid the initial military occupation phase, not so much replacing as reinforcing Red Army jurisdiction, both expanding the range and increasing the depth of Soviet intervention in postwar eastern Europe.

Strategic Insulation

If the internal stimulus of war damage prompted the adoption of economic exploitation, it was the external stimulus of threatened security which effected a new era of strategic insulation for the emerging Soviet Empire.

In a fundamental sense, what came to be called the 'Cold War' in the late 1940s had been implicit ever since the Bolshevik Revolution of October 1917 and became explicit with the establishment of Comintern in March 1919, precipitating a politically bipolar world of ideologically antagonistic camps dedicated to total victory and global supremacy (Roskin, 1994). But the confrontation developed an unprecedented 'chill factor' with the USA's employment of the newly invented atomic bomb to end the Pacific theatre of the Second World War in August 1945. The dropping of 'Big Boy' on Hiroshima established an atomic arsenal club of ultimate exclusivity: the USA was the only member. Such a monopoly in advanced warfare spotlighted the contrast between the two states of East and West conventionally accorded the rank of 'superpower'. The USA had suffered little physical damage and a tolerable level of human casualties in the war whilst gaining enormously in terms of economic and strategic authority, registering a healthy net profit from the Second World War. The Soviet Union had suffered staggering physical and human damage offset only by the modest economic and strategic advantages resulting from its occupation of eastern Europe, registering a debilitating net loss from the war (Kennedy, 1988). While the USA undoubtedly deserved its superpower reputation, Stalin was only too aware of the yawning, perhaps unbridgeable, gap between the Soviet Union's claim to superpower status and the demoralising realities of the Soviet predicament.

How the USA intended to employ (or not to employ) its enhanced global power potential at the close of the Second World War was uncertain. After the First World War, the USA had participated in the Paris Peace Settlement to establish the peacetime geopolitical matrix of interwar Europe, and then withdrew into an isolationism which encouraged the revisionist camp within Versailles Europe to disrupt the new political order. For a year after the end of the Second World War, it seemed as if the USA would repeat its earlier retreat into isolationism: having participated in the Yalta and Potsdam Conferences of 1945, the USA withdrew the bulk of its occupying forces from Europe. Stalin surely breathed a sigh of relief as the military pressure from the Soviet Union's superpower rival was reduced, permitting a relatively relaxed Kremlin attitude towards newly acquired eastern Europe for the year following Potsdam.

From mid-1946, however, the USA returned to Europe, persuaded not to repeat what some condemned as the irresponsible isolationism of the past but instead to employ its superpower authority to advance the ideological cause of pluralism and free enterprise by guaranteeing democratic western Europe. In March 1947, the Truman Doctrine proclaimed American support for global democracy to stabilise a free world assaulted by the tribulations of war (Stokes, 1991). In June 1947, the Marshall Plan promised American financial patronage on an unprecedented scale to shore up a democratic Europe still considered vulnerable to the vestigial Fascist authoritarianism of the right and, in particular, the threatening Communist authoritarianism of the left (Simons, 1993).

Nor was the USA necessarily prepared to rest content with what its principal Soviet expert George Kennan was later to term the 'containment' of Soviet pressure. The 'New Left historians'

were to point out in the 1960s that the American military establishment of the late 1940s contemplated employing its unique
military technology to exploit a strategic 'window of opportunity'
(Lafeber, 1967). Instead of meekly accepting expanded Soviet
jurisdiction, the USA should utilise its atomic monopoly to
promote 'rollback', the expulsion of the Soviet Union from eastern Europe to effect a restoration of interwar Versailles Europe.

As the strategy of the USA moved rapidly after 1945 from
possible isolationism to a 'minimum programme' of 'containment' and later a 'maximum programme' of 'rollback', the reaction of Stalin shifted from relief through concern to alarm
(Dunbabin, 1994). Appreciating the full implications of the
American invention of the atomic bomb, news of which had
been pointedly communicated by Truman at Potsdam, Stalin
made his own atomic bomb the highest priority for Soviet
science in the late 1940s. In the meantime, the vulnerability of
a war-ravaged Soviet Union to American blackmail was self-
evident.

To be forced out of eastern Europe by American 'rollback',
losing access to real estate vital to Soviet economic recovery, was
a grim enough prospect (Roskin, 1994). Yet a still worse nightmare haunted Stalin, a leader whose pervading sense of political
insecurity had already prompted personnel purges claiming or
crippling the lives of millions of Soviet citizens in the 1930s. The
doomsday scenario was that the USA might employ its atomic
power to 'nuke' an effectively defenceless Soviet Union, destroying its great ideological rival by exploiting the unique opportunity
when the discrepancy between American and Soviet power was
greatest. What Nazi Germany had (narrowly) failed to achieve in
the early 1940s, the USA would accomplish in the late 1940s!

The benefit of hindsight allows us the luxury of knowing that
Stalin's fears were exaggerated (Ulam, 1992). The American
'hawks' in the Pentagon may have played extravagant war
games with doomsday and rollback scenarios but they could
never outnumber or overpower the 'doves' reconciled to the
politics of containment. Just as Western war-weariness at
the end of the First World War played a vital role in permitting

the beleaguered Bolshevik regime to survive during 1918–21, so Western war-weariness at the end of the Second World War played a crucial role in letting the devastated Soviet Union off the atomic hook after 1945. Even in a USA becoming increasingly neurotic about Soviet aggression and infiltration, there was no consensus over, still less commitment to, any strategy beyond the containment of the Soviet threat (Dunbabin, 1994).

To Stalin, a politician with no experience and scant knowledge of Western politics, the only prudent response to the rising threat was, first, geopolitical redesigning to enhance Soviet and reduce German power. The jurisdiction of the Soviet Union was extended westward to include the previously independent Baltic states of Estonia, Latvia and Lithuania, as well as eastern Poland, eastern Czechoslovakia and northern Romania. As the Soviet Union grew, so Germany shrank: Poland was bodily shifted over one hundred miles west, exacting territory from Germany in the west in compensation for lands claimed by the Soviet Union in the east. Moreover, to add insult to injury, Germany was not just territorially reduced but also divided and dismembered: four Allied military occupation zones were accepted by Stalin as the means by which the natural superstate of Europe would remain indefinitely crippled, forestalling the possibility of a 'third time lucky' twentieth-century German strike to the east.

Stalin's next preoccupation was to keep the West at arm's length by sealing the frontier of his jurisdiction and converting eastern Europe into a defensive moat or *cordon sanitaire* to preclude another surprise attack (at least by conventional land forces) like that of 1941. An 'Iron Curtain' separating Soviet eastern Europe from the remainder of Europe, announced by Churchill (whether prematurely or prophetically) at Fulton, Missouri, in March 1946, was melodramatically rung down by Stalin in late 1947. The pretext was the availability of Marshall Plan aid to the countries of eastern Europe. The underlying issue was the identification of the frontier between American reach and Soviet control. The test case was the Czechoslovak government's formal application for Marshall Plan financial aid, which was unceremoniously withdrawn under the most intense Soviet pressure in July 1947 (Dunbabin, 1994). The USA may have imposed deliberately inadmissible conditions, calculating that eastern Europe was an economic 'black hole', in order to render acceptance impossible. But whatever the precise apportionment of responsibility between the superpowers, Stalin's suspicion of the Marshall Plan as an economic version of 'rollback' converted the line of demarcation between American influence and Soviet jurisdiction into a permanent political seal.

A new spirit of Soviet-defined conformity swiftly pervaded eastern Europe. Following a Kremlin-organised meeting of representatives of leading European Communist parties at Szklawska Poreba in Poland in September, the Communist Information Bureau (or Cominform) was established in October 1947. In one respect, the Cominform was a predictable successor to the Comintern, temporarily wound up to avoid offending Allied sensibilities in May 1943. Both were international Communist agencies claiming independent authority and legitimacy but actually subservient to Soviet direction and self-interest. In another respect, the two organisations had opposite Soviet-defined objectives: whereas the Comintern had been essentially an offensive, proselytising agency, the Cominform was more a defensive, consolidating organisation. Although including delegates from Western Communist parties not in power, the Cominform was assigned the prime function of promoting a solidarity of communism within an integrated Soviet-led bloc. As eastern Europe was hermetically sealed to prevent the West appreciating the vulnerability of the Soviet regime, the Cominform – the first multinational, 'imperial' institution of the emerging Soviet Empire – was established to foster a Kremlin-defined political homogeneity throughout the jurisdiction of the Soviet Bloc.

Political Subordination

As the internal stimulus of war damage necessitated economic exploitation and the external stimulus of threatened security prompted strategic insulation, a peripheral stimulus of defiance from Yugoslavia accelerated the process by which eastern Europe became totally subordinated to Soviet authority. During 1947–8, the demarcation of the frontier of Kremlin jurisdiction was finally established: the postwar geopolitical settlement of Europe was agreed by the Paris Conference of February 1947 (to take effect in September 1947); Czechoslovakia proved the test-case for the delineation of the frontier with regard to the West in late 1947; but it was Yugoslavia which was to be the test-case for the frontier of the Stalinist empire within Communist eastern Europe over 1948.

Yugoslavia emerged from the Second World War as the most independent-minded of the eastern European states within the still informal Soviet sphere of influence. The geographical location of Yugoslavia, furthest from Russia of the principal eastern European states and with direct access to the Mediterranean, lent a natural potential for geopolitical orientation to either East or West. Despite suffering enormous material and human damage over the 1941–5 period, Yugoslavia survived with an impressive war record. The Communist partisans had conducted a guerrilla war which earned continent-wide pride of place among resistance movements to the Nazi *Neuordnung*. Unlike the remainder of eastern Europe, which had been dependent upon the Red Army for liberation, Yugoslavia achieved self-emancipation from the German yoke, with only a minimal tactical contribution from the Red Army (Tomaszewski, 1989).

Yugoslavia was also the only country of eastern Europe to have a war hero who could make the transition into peacetime statesman. As leader of the partisans, Josip Broz (known as Tito) developed a wartime following which translated in peacetime into a personal popularity virtually unmatched anywhere else in eastern Europe. Tito had also been wily enough to escape the execution which claimed many other agents of the Comintern during the Soviet 'Great Terror' of the late 1930s, and was accordingly pre-conditioned to suspect the motives of Stalin (Auty, 1974). The combination of Yugoslavia's lesser dependence upon the Red Army and Tito's formidable personal authority and deep distrust of Stalin precipitated a fateful confrontation

34

between Belgrade and Moscow which was to prompt the final phase in the emergence of the Stalinist empire.

Even before the establishment of Cominform in October 1947 to orchestrate international Communist solidarity, Tito was showing a marked reluctance to toe the Stalinist line. Stalin demanded that all Communist parties follow the Soviet lead and expected all east European states to accept unconditionally the Soviet model established over the 1930s. Tito viewed Soviet practice as an inspirational example to be adapted where necessary to local east European circumstances and conditions (Ionescu, 1965). While Stalin was increasingly projecting an integrated Soviet Empire in which the countries of eastern Europe were effectively colonies to be exploited for the benefit of the Soviet Union, Tito envisaged a Communist confederation in which the Soviet Union, by dint of size and experience, would be the most influential single member but not to the extent of subordinating smaller components to its exclusive interests.

As early as July 1947, plans were laid at a meeting in Bled between Tito and the Bulgarian Communist leader Georgii Dimitrov for a Yugoslav–Bulgarian federation. The near-coincidence of Tito's Balkan initiative and the American launching of Marshall Aid to eastern Europe represented a double challenge which dominated Soviet defensive strategy after 1947. A furious Stalin found Tito a recalcitrant rebel who refused to obey, or even to negotiate over, Kremlin commands (Roskin, 1994). Despite his initial confident boast that 'I have only to wag my little finger and Tito will fall', Stalin found no body language capable of disciplining his recalcitrant 'disciple'. Unable to back down without irreparable loss of face, Stalin had little choice but to have Yugoslavia expelled from the Cominform in June 1948 (Stokes, 1991).

The 'excommunication' of Yugoslavia from the Communist congregation was a public acknowledgement that neither free negotiation nor macho management could resolve the differences between Stalin and Tito. In order to forestall the accusation that the Cominform was merely a Soviet pawn, it had been agreed in September 1947 that the organisation's headquarters be located not in Moscow but in Belgrade. For the Cominform, convening in June 1948 in the Yugoslav capital, to expel its host country verged on the politically surreal. Moreover, this disciplinary action against Yugoslavia looked embarrassingly like confirmation of the Cominform's alleged puppet status (Ulam, 1992). Outside the political ambit, a Red Army invasion of Yugoslavia to impose Kremlin authority would, in the light of the partisans' formidable reputation as masters of guerrilla warfare, be a risky military enterprise, as well as confirming in the most provocative fashion the expansionist and repressive character of Soviet power (Dunbabin, 1994). Direct Soviet intervention against Yugoslavia was militarily too chancy and politically too damaging to be undertaken.

This demeaning squabble within the 'socialist family of nations' was doubly disastrous to Stalin. That Tito should choose to defy the moral authority of the 'bastion of communism' was bad enough, an unwelcome precedent unsettling to Communist authority throughout the world. That Tito could successfully get away with his defiance of the Kremlin was worse, virtually inciting the other Communist leaders across eastern Europe to follow suit. Dissatisfaction with Soviet authority was by no means limited to Yugoslavia. As early as 1945, the uninhibited rape and pillage indulged in by the Red Army, conspicuously unpunished by Soviet authority, had alienated many east Europeans expecting to welcome their Russian liberators. From 1946, much of eastern Europe had been irremediably antagonised by Soviet asset-stripping, leading to a groundswell of anti-Russian resentment in 1947–8 (Roskin, 1994). Yugoslavia's sensational escape from Soviet jurisdiction was bound to have both an inspiration effect and a demonstration effect across the whole of eastern Europe.

Successful Yugoslav defiance constituted a peripheral stimulus provoking an immediate and profound core reaction from the Kremlin. To prevent the spread of 'Titoism' from Yugoslavia, threatening the loss of all recently acquired eastern Europe, Stalin had no alternative but to crack down throughout a Soviet Empire entering its final constructive phase of political subordination (Ulam, 1992).

Three consecutive stages in the Soviet disciplining of eastern Europe may be identified as typical (Seton-Watson, 1956). The first was a process by which genuine coalitions of Communist and non-Communist parties were forcibly converted into façade coalitions in which the Communists held the effective power. At Moscow's insistence, the crucial portfolio of minister of the interior was always reserved for a Communist, so that non-Communist representation could be whittled down to a merely cosmetic level as a tokenist tactic by the increasingly authoritarian Communist establishments.

The second stage saw the bogus coalitions purged of all non-Communists to establish a Communist monopoly of power. This monopolisation was sometimes effected through what the Hungarian Communist leader Matyas Rakosi once termed the 'salami tactics' of political manoeuvre, usually by branding non-Communists as Nazi collaborators (Morris, 1984). On other occasions, naked force or 'direct action' was employed: for example, the arranged 'accidental death' in March 1948 of the spiritedly anti-Communist Czechoslovak foreign minister Jan Masaryk (Schopflin, 1993).

The third stage, prompted by fear of the spread of the Titoist heresy, was a full-scale inquisition which purged the all-Communist establishments of any elements regarded as unreliable in their unconditional allegiance to the Kremlin line. To tackle or pre-empt a 'revolt of the first secretaries', a series of show-trials claimed the lives of a succession of high-flying bosses, from Laszlo Rajk and Traicho Kostov in Hungary and Bulgaria in 1949, through Rudolf Slansky and Vladimir Clementis in Czechoslovakia in 1952 to Lucretiu Patrascanu in Romania in 1954 (Tismaneanu, 1992). Below the level of the élite, an estimated one-quarter of the bureaucratic cadres and Communist party rank-and-file suffered execution, imprisonment or dismissal over the half-decade following 1948 (Morris, 1984).

There appear to have been two Soviet models for the systematic disciplining of the east European Communist parties. The Stalinist 'Great Terror' of the late 1930s, which claimed such illustrious 'Old Bolshevik' luminaries as Nikolai Bukharin, plainly provided the precedent and pattern for the show-trials of the late 1940s. The Red Army takeover and subordination into a puppet state of Mongolia after July 1921 supplied an Asian blueprint for the postwar, wider-ranging European purge (Dalziel, 1993). Soviet practices of the 1920s and 1930s were the models for the Soviet-inspired 'mongolisation' and 'terrorisation' of eastern Europe in the late 1940s.

Typically, but not invariably, 'Muscovites' or Moscow-trained Communists survived the purges at the expense of 'Nationalists' or indigenous Communists who (like Tito himself) had always been tempted to place local considerations above the demands of Soviet-determined doctrine (Morris, 1984). The often indiscriminate, sometimes apparently random choice of victims may suggest that innocence and guilt were only tangential to the purge exercise. The principal objective of such 'quota culling' was less to target and eradicate a guilty minority than to terrorise the surviving majority into abject servility (Schopflin, 1993). Whatever the precise dynamics of purge, the consequences were plain: in different places and on varying time-scales between 1947 and 1954, eastern Europe was purged of any leaders of the most passing resemblance to the renegade Tito, who were replaced by Kremlin quislings unconditionally obedient to Soviet authority, heading 'People's Democracies' determined by the established Stalinist template.

Ideological Conversion

Over the half-decade following the end of the Second World War, three stimuli – internal, external and peripheral – forced eastern Europe through four broadly sequential, though often overlapping, cumulative phases of growing Soviet control. Without denying the relevance of military, economic, strategic and political factors in the construction of the new eastern European order, the contemporary official Soviet line, however, insisted on the primacy of ideological motivation, a bold claim which the historian cannot allow to pass uninvestigated.

Ever since the inspirational October Revolution of 'Petrograd 1917', the Bolshevik state and (after 1924) the Soviet Union had portrayed itself as the bastion of communism from which ideological expansionism to effect a world socialist revolution would eventually be achieved. The Comintern was created in 1919 for the dedicated purpose of promoting socialist revolution in the wider capitalist world. Trotsky had proclaimed that the success of communism in Russia depended upon the victory of the world socialist revolution: without that crucial broader dimension, the Russian Revolution would become more and more Russian but less and less revolutionary, disgracing the international socialist movement by its shortcomings. Although the Comintern was originally established out of disappointment at the reluctance of international revolution to occur spontaneously, and although the proselytising performance and achievement of the Comintern in interwar Europe was embarrassingly poor, the Soviet propaganda of the late 1940s consistently presented the expansion of Soviet authority across eastern Europe as a victory for the ideological dynamic of communism.

Little evidence exists to suggest that the ideological factor loomed large in the Stalinist decision-making process (Ulam, 1992). The dating of the point at which the ideological element lost out to other considerations has often been debated. A popular date is May 1943, when Stalin's closure of the Comintern to avoid offending his capitalist allies-in-arms may be interpreted as symbolic of the primacy of expediency over ideology. Many would argue that the 'Great Terror' of the 1930s eliminated the 'Old Bolsheviks' *en masse*, replacing a whole generation of zealots animated by 'creed' with new cadres of opportunist and careerist 'October Bolsheviks' motivated by 'greed'. Others would suggest a much earlier date, arguing that the traumatic experience of the civil war over 1918–21 effectively robbed the Old Bolsheviks of their ideological virginity. A few would go so far as to suggest that the predominance of the ideological motivator among Bolsheviks even before October 1917 has been much exaggerated.

Consensus is almost complete, however, on the judgement that the creed factor of ideological commitment was a principal casualty of the Soviet experience, overwhelmed by the greed factor of political ambition and the need factor of practical necessity. Although lip-service to ideological justification was punctiliously maintained at the level of public propaganda, the post-1945 construction of the Soviet empire was overwhelmingly dictated by a complex of military, economic, strategic and political considerations.

But while the ideological motivator may have counted for little in the Soviet Union of the late 1940s, its role in eastern Europe should not be entirely discounted. It is true that some countries of eastern Europe (like Hungary and Poland) had little or no sympathy for communism after the Second World War; but others (like Czechoslovakia, Bulgaria and Yugoslavia) demonstrated a substantial degree of support for, or even commitment to, communism (Tampke, 1983). For example, the Communist party enjoyed considerable popular support in Czechoslovakia throughout the interwar period, and in the democratically run general election of May 1946, the Communists secured 38 per cent of the total vote to become the largest Czechoslovak parliamentary party (Swain, 1993: 48).

More generally, a part-ideological, part-humanitarian respect for the Soviet Union pervaded much of eastern Europe. Many considered that, by first abandoning eastern Europe to the Depression and then adopting the repressive and warmongering shape of fascism, capitalism had disgraced itself, suffering a moral bankruptcy which favoured the socialist alternative (Crampton, 1994: 213). With three-quarters of all German casualties in the Second World War incurred on the Eastern Front, the Soviet Union was perceived as deserving the ultimate credit for defeating Nazi Germany, at an unprecedented self-sacrificing cost to itself unmatched by any other combatant. Moreover, such was the scale of physical damage caused by the war that, at the most practical level, capitalism was simply not up to the task of peacetime recovery: only Soviet-style state planning could hope to cope with a postwar challenge of such magnitude.

Thus, while socialist ideology may have disappeared as a motivator within the Soviet Union by 1945, being largely replaced by official nationalism over the Second World War, its appeal across much of eastern Europe was significant enough to be exploited by Stalin in the construction of his Soviet Empire. Whether eastern Europeans would now experience a mass conversion to the newly established, officially promoted Communist creed, or would soon prove as ideologically indifferent as their Soviet counterparts had already become, remained to be seen.

The Newest Empire

The newly constructed Soviet Empire faced the second half of the twentieth century with many outward indicators of success. The jurisdiction of the pre-1939 Soviet Union had been recovered: Ukraine and Belorussia, temporarily lost to German occupation in 1941–4, had been reclaimed, with the opportunity seized over the late 1940s to liquidate local nationalists as fascist collaborators (notably by Stalin's 'Butcher of Ukraine', Nikita Khrushchev). Moreover, the postwar Soviet Union was significantly larger than the interwar Soviet Union, now incorporating the Baltic states of Estonia, Latvia and Lithuania, eastern Poland, the eastern Czechoslovakian region of Ruthenia and the northern Romanian region of Bessarabia, to become effectively a restoration of the expanded Soviet Union agreed by Stalin and Hitler in 1939–40.

In addition, the Soviet Union now dominated a Soviet Bloc which included most of eastern Europe, a sphere experiencing Soviet jurisdiction for the first time. In the sense that the east European member-states were predominantly not volunteers but conscripts, dependent and subordinate 'satellites' of the Soviet Union, the Bloc constituted a Soviet Empire geared to the exclusive interests of the Soviet Union (Seton-Watson, 1961). The lesser empire of the prewar Soviet Union had grown into the greater empire of the Soviet Bloc, albeit zoned between the inner empire of an extended Soviet Union and the outer empire of an eastern Europe undergoing a Sovietisation rigorous enough to threaten 'an end to diversity' (Swain, 1993: 56). In simplistic cartographic terms at least, the success of the postwar Soviet Union was self-evident: the Soviet Bloc constituted the largest land empire in history.

Unrevealed by the 1950 atlas was a new territorial self-confidence on the part of the Soviet Union. In September 1949, the first Soviet atomic bomb was successfully exploded, a military turning-point which effectively slammed the strategic window of opportunity available to the USA since mid-1945. With the 'atomic club' now numbering two members, the USA lost the overwhelming military initiative of the past four years. The opportunistic 'rollback' option became redundant over-night, to be replaced by the infinitely more modest 'contain-ment' strategy which was to be the foundation of American policy towards the Soviet Bloc for the rest of its forty-year career. As the Cold War stabilised and even became institutio-nalised, the Soviet Union could now claim (if without total conviction) approximate parity with the USA in military tech-nology, an achievement which brought general acknowledge-ment of its genuine superpower status and a new sense of domestic and international security for the Soviet Empire.

There were, nevertheless, features already undermining con-fidence in the long-term prospects of the Soviet Empire. The creation of the Empire over the extraordinarily short period of some five years testified both to its essentially *ad hoc* nature and its unacceptably rushed construction. A close investigation of the 1944–9 period suggests an adventitious process of pragmatic reaction to exigent stimuli rather than the execution of a pre-designed master-plan for the incorporation and homogenisation of eastern Europe (Polonsky, 1975). Admittedly, Stalin was deter-mined from 1944 at the very latest to control Poland, which he regarded as the West's natural invasion route to the Soviet Union and therefore the key to peacetime Soviet security (Young, 1991). But Stalin was initially relatively flexible in his strategy towards the rest of eastern Europe, insisting that the Soviet Union alone among the Great Powers had the right to consider eastern Europe as its exclusive sphere of influence but not necessarily convinced of the advisability or necessity of Soviet intervention to create a sealed and secure Soviet Empire (Simons, 1993). In August 1946, for instance, Stalin was still accepting the principle of 'different roads to socialism' across eastern Europe (Swain, 1993). The Soviet Empire positioned by 1950 was less constructed by premeditated, ideological architect-design than precipitated by compelling military, economic, strategic and political factors combining into an accelerating and increasingly irresistible chain-reaction.

The near-desperate efforts of Stalin to bluff his way out of an extraordinarily perilous predicament were often more successful than they deserved. For example, contemporary Western opinion regarded the dramatic Berlin air-lift of June 1948 to September 1949 as the defining episode of staunch resistance to Communist threat, failing to appreciate that Stalin's bold feint may have been blocked but he had won the opening round in the confrontation contest (Kennedy, 1988). And yet the vulnerability of the new empire showed. The ringing-down of the Iron Curtain, for instance, regarded in 1947 as proof (should proof be needed) of Stalin's awesome power, appears in retrospect to have been less a demonstration of strength than a confession of weakness. The impudent defiance of the Kremlin by Tito in 1948 exposed more than any other episode the limitations on Stalinist authority, compelling Stalin either to resign himself to the loss of eastern Europe or to undertake an immediate clampdown to secure his westerly acquisitions (Ulam, 1992). Even so, the reputation of Titoist Yugoslavia as 'the one that got away' endured long after the death of Stalin, a perpetual incitement to would-be eastern European decolonisers throughout the lifetime of the Soviet Empire. Among the events of the critical year 1948, it was Belgrade rather than Berlin which revealed most about, and determined the development of, the Soviet Empire.

Finally, the Soviet Empire was under construction at a time of incipient global decolonisation. The precipitate British withdrawal from India, the 'jewel in the crown' of the British Empire, in 1947, signalled a general recognition that the Second World War had strained the overseas empires of the western European states to the point that withdrawal from imperial commitments would be an irresistible and accelerating feature of the postwar world. As so often in its history, backward Russia found itself entering a developmental phase just as its more advanced rivals moved on to the next phase. Although the creation of an eastern European empire made short-term sense in the uniquely disadvantaged circumstances of Russia in the late 1940s, its anachronistic timing within the global setting raised fundamental questions about the empire's medium-term viability and ultimate longevity. How long could this 'jerrybuilt edifice, ramshackle and extemporised', a hastily manufactured product of the Second World War and the Cold War, buck the global trend towards decolonisation? (Fernandez-Armesto, 1995: 187) Certainly the newest empire, was the Soviet Bloc also destined to be the last, and consequently (in all probability) the shortest-lived empire of modern times?

3

BUDAPEST 1956: THAW
AND REFREEZE

The decade of the 1950s brought fundamental challenge to a Stalinist empire which had only recently been established and was still in the process of consolidation. In this respect, while an event of enormous symbolic importance, the death on 5 March 1953 of Stalin, the architect of the Soviet Empire, was less a political watershed in Yalta Europe than at first appears. The year 1953 did not mark a neat hiatus between an era of consolidation of the Stalinist empire and an era of challenge to a post-Stalinist empire: at the time of Stalin's death, the consolidation of the empire was still incomplete; and challenge to the empire was already under way.

The imperial consolidation process had been initiated politically by the creation of Cominform in October 1947 and was reinforced by the formation of Comecon (Council for Mutual Economic Assistance) in January 1949, originally designed as an instrument of concerted economic boycott against rebel Yugoslavia (Simons, 1993). Socially and culturally, however, the integration of the People's Democracies of eastern Europe into the Soviet-dominated Communist Bloc was only beginning. Moreover, military consolidation was conspicuously stalled: partly because no one could doubt the practical hegemony of the Soviet Army, there was no sense of urgency to elaborate an overall formal structure to define the relationships between the various military forces of the Soviet Bloc. The full range of imperial institutions was thus demonstrably incomplete at the time of Stalin's death: the Soviet Empire was still in the making in 1953.

Although opposition to the Stalinist regime within the Soviet Empire had been fundamentally eliminated through purges and intimidation by 1953, external challenge across the broader Communist camp was already well-rooted. The defiance of Tito in 1948, and the spectre of 'national communism' raised by the defection of Yugoslavia, played a crucial role in Stalin's crackdown on his remaining jurisdiction. Soviet acquisition of the atomic bomb in September 1949 and covert prosecution of a war by proxy in the shape of the Korean War after June 1950 convinced Tito that a newly ebullient Soviet Bloc might entertain thoughts of intervention against Yugoslavia, thereby confirming and broadening the Yugoslav–Soviet rift. In reality, the Korean War probably acted to Tito's advantage: although to suggest that 'Korea saved Yugoslavia' would be exaggerated, Stalin's perennial concern to avoid the nightmare of a two-front war safeguarded Tito at a time when his own regime was still consolidating.

Elsewhere in the West, the international socialist movement was self-interestedly more sympathetic to Titoist 'national communism' than to Stalinist 'monolithic communism', as articulated by the Italian Communist leader Palmiro Togliatti's expedient doctrine of 'polycentrism' (Dunbabin, 1994). Nor was dissent restricted to Europe: while Tito to the West overtly defied Stalinist authority, the creation to the East in 1949 of the Communist China of Mao Tse-tung, soon anticipating 'the blossoming of a hundred flowers of socialism', augured a future superpower unlikely to rest content with subordinate status within a Soviet-dominated Communist Bloc.

From Stalin to Khrushchev

With imperial consolidation incomplete and imperial challenge already mounting, the death of Stalin constituted an unwelcome early crisis for the vulnerable Soviet Empire. Two features dominated the immediate issue of post-Stalinist succession: whether loved or loathed, Stalin had so dominated Soviet politics for the last quarter-century that he was the hardest possible act to follow; and the seventy-three-year-old Stalin had obstinately designated no successor, even taking a malicious delight in keeping likely runners in the succession stakes guessing. From the instant of Stalin's long-awaited death, a leadership struggle was inevitable.

In the run-up to 1953, there were four top-level candidates who could be construed as 'crown princes' jostling for the Stalinist succession: the ultra hard-line Andrei Zhdanov, who had seemed to be Stalin's preferred choice but who died (under mysterious circumstances) in August 1948; Georgii Malenkov, who represented the Soviet *apparat* (state bureaucracy) and became the favourite to succeed Stalin in 1952; Lavrentii Beria, who wielded formidable backstairs influence as head of the state security forces; and the most senior CPSU official, Nikita Khrushchev, who had only recently been recruited from the provinces and was therefore something of an unknown, or at least under-regarded, political quantity (Keep, 1995).

Immediately on Stalin's death, a 'collective leadership' was announced, which could be variously interpreted as a fulsome tribute to Stalin (in that no single successor could possibly fill his massive shoes) or a tacit indicator that a departure from the autocratic centralisation of Stalinism was desirable. In practice, the 'collective leadership' proved to be not a permanent semi-constitutional arrangement but a temporary façade behind which a vicious power struggle was waged over 1953–5.

Despite the universal and keen sense of loss occasioned by the demise of Stalin, the leadership struggle was premised upon the desirability, even the necessity of a break with (at very least) the worst excesses of Stalinist authoritarianism. Heading the security forces in their various manifestations and under their various euphemistic titles since 1938, Beria most conspicuously represented the now-unacceptable face of Stalinism and predictably became the first casualty in the power struggle. A bold (or

desperate) attempt by Beria to fabricate some reformist credentials backfired, antagonising the East German leader Walter
Ulbricht and provoking popular disturbances in East Berlin in
June 1953. Outmanoeuvred by Malenkov and Khrushchev
working in conspiratorial concert, Beria suffered summary
execution in December 1953 (McCauley, 1981; Keep, 1995).

Malenkov and Khrushchev (by now First Secretary of the
CPSU) next embarked upon a competition not only to win
support within the Soviet establishment but to curry favour
among the broader populace. That both rivals should seek to
recommend themselves to wider society was both a tacit
acknowledgement that neither could ever expect to match the
personal autocracy of Stalin and a public recognition that the
Stalinist legacy had to be adapted to changing circumstances
(Schopflin, 1993). After the 'Second Revolution' and 'Great
Terror' of the 1930s, the almost indescribable carnage of the
'Great Fatherland War' and the privations of the postwar decade, the Soviet population deserved and expected material
reward in the shape of a dramatically improved quality of life.

The similarities in the campaigns of Malenkov and Khrushchev were infinitely more significant than their differences. Both
preached a 'thaw' in the Stalin-chilled domestic and international political climates. At home, the liquidation of Beria signalled a less repressive era of greater freedom of speech, reduced
censorship and the release of most political prisoners from the
Stalinist *gulag* (security camps). Abroad, a new policy of *détente*
with the West permitted a responsible shifting of state resources
away from armaments and heavy industry towards consumer
industries, raising the prospect of the availability of refrigerators,
TVs and eventually cars as a belated reward for the postwar
Soviet generation.

Khrushchev won the leadership struggle on three distinct but
related fronts. On the 'constitutional front', he asserted (or rather
reclaimed) the moral authority of the Communist party over the
apparat. During and after the Second World War, the practical
power of the administrative cadres had grown immensely in
response to the demands of the war effort and postwar recovery.

By contrast, the authority of the CPSU had stalled, even faded: less reliable personnel inducted in wartime to effect a broader 'party of heroes' were purged away again by Zhdanov in the late 1940s, leaving the party dazed and demoralised. Under licence from Stalin, Khrushchev set out to reassert the traditional party monopoly of moral authority over the encroachments of the *apparat* (Hosking, 1985). Over 1953–5, Khrushchev attacked the 'anti-Party' elements in the Soviet establishment, securing the reluctant submission of the *apparat* (as represented by Malenkov) to the ideological authority of the CPSU.

On the domestic front, Khrushchev pursued his de-Stalinisation campaign more imaginatively than Malenkov. The publicity-conscious Khrushchev promoted daring new projects like the initially spectacular if ultimately flawed 'Virgin Lands Scheme' in Soviet central Asia, pledged to boldly going where no arable farmer had gone before (McCauley, 1981). Espousing causes which portrayed him as an authentic 'man of the people', Khrushchev sought out photo opportunities in which he unblushingly appeared as a proletarian among proletarians one day and a peasant among peasants the next. Khrushchev was infinitely more at home in the new quasi-populist politics of the post-Stalin era than the narrowly bureaucratic Malenkov.

Khrushchev was also impressive on the diplomatic front. Condemning the 'Two Camp Doctrine' of inevitable conflict between capitalism and communism as preached by Zhdanov in the late 1940s, Khrushchev argued the viability of 'Peaceful Coexistence' between East and West: although capitalism and communism were by their very natures in perennial competition, their trajectories could become essentially parallel, with no fatally unavoidable collision course or certainty of apocalypse (Crankshaw, 1984). Like Stalin's earlier 'Socialism in One Country' slogan, Khrushchev's 'Peaceful Coexistence' stratagem deftly adapted orthodox Communist doctrine to the exigencies of the present, securing a broad consensus of support within the CPSU without outraging too many die-hard traditionalists.

Khrushchev's fundamental motivation for his determined (and what his enemies would later condemn as reckless) de-Stalinisation seems to have been personal ambition for power rather than ideological distaste for Stalinism as such. Khrushchev had, after all, only risen to striking distance of supreme power though uncritical obedience to Stalin: with an unenviable reputation for doing some of Stalin's dirtiest work (notably as the 'Butcher of the Ukraine' in the late 1940s), Khrushchev had made his mark as one of Stalin's deadliest troubleshooters. The exacting demands of post-Stalinist power politics now induced Khrushchev, hitherto almost more Stalinist than Stalin, to undergo the speediest of conversions on the hazardous Damascus road to his career summit.

After ousting Malenkov from the premiership in February 1955, Khrushchev demonstrated his domination of Soviet policy by pursuit of a de-Stalinisation which manifested itself in a flurry of mixed, even contradictory signals which first bemused, then encouraged and finally dismayed both the West and the colonies of the Soviet Empire. Over the early summer of 1955, three events cumulatively set all of eastern Europe buzzing with speculation about the future of the Soviet Bloc.

In May 1955, the Soviet Army evacuated its Austrian occupation zone, part of a multinational agreement by which all four Allied armies withdrew to leave an independent neutral state of Austria (Dunbabin, 1994). The implications of the disengagement were enormous. This first (and until 1989 only) example of voluntary Soviet withdrawal from conquered territory contradicted the conventional wisdom in the West that the expansionist Soviet Union never retreated, a staple of the Cold War mindset (Ionescu, 1965). If Khrushchev was prepared to withdraw from Austria to demonstrate his public faith in 'Peaceful Coexistence', would he concede further? Was Germany, partitioned like Austria into Allied occupation zones since 1945, the next on the liberation list? If 'Austria 1955' was not just a diplomatic gesture to the current 'spirit of Geneva' but a political test-case, could all eastern Europe expect a voluntary decolonisation of the recently established Soviet Empire in the foreseeable future?

Apparently contradicting this optimistic scenario was the almost simultaneous signing, in May 1955, of the Warsaw Pact.

In the short term, the creation of the Pact was a Soviet response to the admission of the Federal Republic of Germany into membership of NATO (Fejto, 1974). In the long term, the Pact constituted the last remaining, that is to say military, component in the array of imperial institutions created over 1947–55 to effect full control of the Soviet Empire. In the medium term, the establishment of the Warsaw Pact was intended to demonstrate that the withdrawal from Austria was an exceptional, one-off gesture of goodwill: the remainder of eastern Europe would stay within a territorially concentrated, organisationally refurbished and permanent Soviet Empire.

The final episode was Khrushchev's visit to Belgrade in May–June 1955, following which a public apology was extended to Tito for Stalin's past treatment of Yugoslavia. Whether the meeting represented a genuine reconciliation or an expedient accommodation between Soviet and Yugoslav viewpoints, the announcement spawned almost endless speculation. If Khrushchev's apology meant that Stalin had been mistaken and Tito correct, the implications for the moral legitimacy of the Communist establishments were fundamental (Fejto, 1974). If Stalin had been wrong, what was the justification for the wave of anti-Titoist purges which had decimated every east European Communist party over the last seven years? If Tito was right, then 'national communism' was legitimised internationally, beaming a green light to Titoism across the Soviet Empire. Intended to draw Yugoslavia back into the 'socialist family of nations', Khrushchev's apology to 'the first heretic' succeeded only in legitimising 'national communism' and delegitimising the present Communist establishments (Ulam, 1992). Throughout eastern Europe, surviving 'national Communists' were encouraged to follow Yugoslavia's example while confused or embarrassed resident establishments underwent a crisis of conscience and legitimacy.

The first months of 1956 served only to reinforce the sense of mandate for change within the Soviet Empire. At the XX Congress of the CPSU in February 1956, Khrushchev delivered a so-called 'Secret Speech' denouncing Stalin and much of his record of achievement. The speech may have been secret (or rather confidential) in the sense that it was intended for the party faithful rather than the general public, but its official provenance and sensational message ensured a national (and soon a global) resonance amounting to 'a veritable revolution' (Hosking, 1985: 337). The furore engendered by this political bombshell reverberated through eastern Europe, promoting a social climate in which radical reform was perceived as not just possible or desirable but actually imperative (Tomaszewski, 1989).

As if to confirm Khrushchev's admission of the illegitimacy of the Stalinist empire, Cominform was disbanded in April 1956. With the political imperial institution of the Soviet Empire closed down after less than a decade, ostensibly as a handsome gesture of apology to Yugoslavia, fundamental change seemed inescapable (Ionescu, 1965). In the same month, the Soviet delegation at the Bandung Conference on colonialism subscribed to the principles of national independence, popular self-determination and prohibition of external intervention. Formally endorsed by the Soviet government in July 1956, Kremlin commitment to global decolonisation of empire was now on the international record, propelling the dismantling of the Soviet Empire to the top of the eastern European political agenda.

Polish October, Hungarian November

The decisions consciously (if not necessarily prudently) taken by Khrushchev in the imperial capital during 1955–6 were interpreted by eastern Europe as the collective green light for, at very least, a federalisation of the Soviet Empire into a 'socialist commonwealth' legitimised by Titoist 'national communism'. Given the growing sense of national euphoria sweeping eastern Europe, a full-scale decolonisation of the Soviet Empire was not considered beyond the bounds of geopolitical possibility.

The lead in responding to the Kremlin's initiatives was taken by the largest state in eastern Europe, Poland. The very fact of Poland's geopolitical size and demographic weight meant that Poland was the most important single colony in the Empire and would therefore be treated with self-interested circumspection by Soviet authority. In February 1956, the hard-line Stalinist Polish leader Boleslaw Bierut died, to be replaced by the more lenient Edward Ochab. In June 1956, workers' demonstrations in Poznan posted warning that the de-Stalinisation promoted by Khrushchev from Moscow could destabilise Poland, raising the spectre of a revisionist brush-fire spreading across all eastern Europe (Simons, 1993).

On this occasion, however, Poland was not to be the test-case for the retention of the Soviet Empire. The principal responsibility for this Polish non-event lay with the new Communist first secretary Wladyslaw Gomulka. Purged in the Stalin-inspired anti-Titoist drive of 1948, Gomulka was fortunate to survive to be allowed to return to the leadership of the Polish Communist party by Khrushchev in mid-October 1956 (Bethell, 1972). This permission was among Khrushchev's few adroit actions of 1956, for Gomulka both commanded the respect of the majority of Poles and was prepared to settle for concessions to Polish-style national communism rather than risk a more adventurous strategy. To Gomulka, Poland's geographical location between the Soviet Union and Germany, with no non-Communist neighbours, amounted to a geopolitical predicament which rendered a drive for full independence suicidally unrealistic (Ionescu, 1965).

In a spirit of opportunistic reformism, Gomulka adopted the modest Yugoslav model of strategy, negotiating with Khrushchev for major Soviet concessions to Poland within a more devolved imperial jurisdiction (Swain, 1993). By mid-November, Gomulka had secured substantive gains: the cancellation of Poland's existing debts to the Soviet Union, new preferential trade terms and extended credits with the Soviet Union, abandonment of the hated Soviet-imposed collectivisation of Polish agriculture and significant concessions to the autonomy of the Roman Catholic church in Poland (Ulam, 1992). Though lacking traditional Polish-flavoured drama and heroism, the 'Polish October' effectively raised Poland from a colony to a dominion of the Soviet Empire.

The principal reason why Khrushchev was prepared to accommodate Gomulka, other than the relative restraint of Polish demands, was his need to buy off Poland in order to concentrate upon the crisis of 'Spring in October' in Hungary (Ionescu, 1965: 58). Why it should be Hungary, the smallest of the Soviet satellites, which proved to be the flash-point of 1956 resulted from a combination of historical, geographical and political factors. In the first place, Hungary was a non-Slav enclave in the overwhelmingly Slav landscape of eastern Europe, with a racial antagonism towards the Russians sharpened by such historical episodes as the tsarist suppression of the Hungarian bid for independence headed by Lajos Kossuth and Sandor Petofi in 1849 (Molnar, 1971). Moreover, since the Second World War, Hungary had been treated exceptionally harshly by Soviet power, partly because of the relative abundance of its exploitable resources, partly as deliberate punishment for its expedient alliance with Nazi Germany over the decade before 1945. Resentment against Soviet extortion and repression, universal throughout eastern Europe, was nowhere greater than in Hungary.

Against this background, the Communist establishment in Hungary was particularly vulnerable in 1956. Following an ephemeral Hungarian Socialist Republic led by Bela Kun which lasted some five months in 1919, a 'White Terror' effectively purged Hungary of Communists throughout the interwar period. As a consequence, the Soviet determination to concoct an amenable Hungarian Communist establishment after 1945 ran into considerable practical difficulties of recruitment. As late as 1956, the Hungarian Communist party was proportionately the smallest among the Soviet satellites, attracting general scorn as a gang of cynical opportunists and shameless self-servers, many of whom were not even ethnically Hungarian. From March 1956, the self-constituted Petofi Circle served as a forum for impassioned debate about the future of Hungary, and then as an alternative parliament of the Hungarian intelligentsia, attracting a popular legitimacy which patently embarrassed the Communist establishment (Ionescu, 1965). Polarised by a bitter, ongoing feud between the hardline Stalinist Matyas Rakosi and the reformist Imre Nagy, the Hungarian Communist party was fatally flawed as crisis loomed over 1956 (Molnar, 1971).

With the summer of 1956 came a climate of opinion which readily assumed that Hungary's defining moment of destiny had arrived. While Poland was settling for the modest objective of greater autonomy within the Soviet Empire, Hungary spared the Yugoslav model the briefest of considerations before adopting the ambitious Austrian model of complete independence. A glance at the map of Yalta Europe boosted Hungarian self-confidence: after the concessions to Yugoslavia, Hungary's southern neighbour, and the withdrawal from Austria, Hungary's western neighbour, Hungary herself was indisputably next in line geopolitically. Soviet withdrawal from Hungary was the logical next instalment in a voluntary 'rollback' from the western periphery of the Soviet Empire, a territorial shrinkage of Soviet jurisdiction which would precipitate an independent Hungary if only Hungarians pressed their national cause (Molnar, 1971; Schopflin, 1993). Future generations would not forgive the Hungarians of 1956 if they neglected to act at this supremely propitious historical juncture.

Through the late summer and autumn of 1956, the situation in Hungary became explosive. Under pressure from Khrushchev, the provocatively Stalinist Rakosi was forced out of power in July but his compromise successor Erno Gero failed to calm or channel the rising demands of the mobilised Hungarian intelligentsia, youth and workers. By September, the broad Hungarian reform movement was out of control, demanding the immediate renunciation of Soviet links and proclamation of the independence of Hungary (Molnar, 1971). In a desperate last attempt to stabilise the deteriorating situation, the reformist Nagy was returned to the leadership of the Hungarian Communist party in late October. But the hapless Nagy enjoyed the support of neither the Communist establishment nor the reform movement, a politically untenable position which could only exacerbate the collapsing relations between Hungary and the Soviet Union (Ionescu, 1965).

Hesitantly over late October and decisively in early November 1956, the Soviet Army intervened to crush by military force what became the 'Hungarian Uprising' (Molnar, 1971). The Soviet

rationale for armed intervention combined domestic and international considerations. Ostensibly, the Soviet Army was 'assist-
ing the fraternal government' of Hungary in resolving a law-and-
order problem which had got beyond the capability of the local
authority to tackle, an argument which was not altogether untrue
(Tampke, 1983). More profoundly, by late 1956 Hungary was
animated by an ungovernable nationalism which not only contradicted the letter and spirit of communism but threatened the
geopolitical integrity of the entire Soviet Bloc. Fearing another
subversive 'Belgrade 1948', Moscow felt compelled to crack
down on Hungary in 1956 in order to prevent a domino effect
of nationalist rebellion which would fatally damage the Soviet
Empire.

Internationally, the Kremlin trembled for the security of its
western frontier, opened to redefinition through its recognition of
Austria and Yugoslavia in 1955. To withdraw voluntarily for
diplomatic advantage as in 1955 was quite different from retreating ignominiously under popular duress in 1956. Alarmed by the
memory of the recent Korean War, Moscow feared either out-
right expulsion from Hungary or the humiliating scenario of
Hungary as a 'European Korea' partitioned between East and
West. A final consideration for Moscow was the timing of suppression. Under normal circumstances, military action from the
West in support of national defiance of Communist power, while
not likely, could not be entirely excluded. But the coincidental
eruption of the Suez Crisis was diverting and splitting the West,
rendering a united and effective military Western response to the
Soviet clampdown in Hungary impractical. Although it would be
a gross exaggeration to suggest that 'Suez doomed Hungary',
Western preoccupation with the Middle East certainly undermined the Kremlin 'doves' with their counsels of caution and
compromise, and favoured the insistence of the Kremlin 'hawks'
on prompt Soviet military action against Hungary.

Hungary was occupied and bloodily repressed by the Soviet
Army in late 1956, with a total death toll estimated at up to
25 000 (Fejto, 1974). Seeking opportunities unavailable in Hungary or fearing reprisals from the restored Communist regime

headed by Janos Kadar, a further 200 000 chose to escape to the West, a damaging exodus comprising the largest and fastest European population movement of the 1950s. The first attempt at overt defection from the Soviet Empire was unceremoniously crushed by naked military imperial power before a news-hungry, media-informed international audience. Throughout an eastern Europe which felt more captive than ever before, the 'Hungarian November' of 1956 was instantly enshrined as the 'new 1849' for the reactionary Soviet Empire, now vilified as the twentieth-century successor to the tsarist 'prison of nations'.

Reaction and Readjustment

'1956' reverberated through the Soviet Empire for the next four years, setting a reactionary tone of re-Stalinisation (or neo-Stalinisation) and, less predictably, prompting a fundamental shift in the nature of imperial jurisdiction through the Soviet Union and eastern Europe.

In strategic terms, Hungary in 1956 had proved the unsuccessful test-case for the decolonisation of the Soviet Empire in eastern Europe. '1956' demonstrated that the Soviet Empire was a permanent fixture: the Kremlin would be undertaking no territorial downsizing, no voluntary 'rollback' from eastern Europe. The Hungarian tactic of defiance of imperial authority was discredited: the 'Hungarian November' showed that the effective support of the West could not be relied upon (notwithstanding the sabre-rattling assurances of the US Secretary of State John Foster Dulles since 1953), while Hungary alone was simply too small to defy Soviet might (Molnar, 1971; Roskin, 1994). In contrast, the Polish policy of negotiation with imperial authority was endorsed: as 'a revolution channelled', the 'Polish October' had secured substantive improvements in the position of Poland (Fejto, 1974: 100). The ringing lesson of 1956 was that the future line of eastern Europe should not be suicidal rebellion in the pursuit of independence but opportunistic pressure for greater autonomy within a more devolved imperial structure.

Militarily, '1956' prompted the immediate and rigorous clamping of an 'iron ring' across the entire Soviet Bloc to forestall any spread of the Hungarian spirit of heroic resistance (Simons, 1993: 106). More generally, the 'Hungarian November' re-emphasised the ultimate dependence of the Soviet Empire on military power, boosting the political role of the armed forces within the imperial establishment. In the longer term, '1956' also promoted a closer integration of the armed forces of the Soviet Bloc. It was embarrassing that a military intervention officially justified as the joint and collective action of the 'fraternal members of the socialist family of nations' should in reality be undertaken by the Soviet Army alone (an unavoidable gaffe which was not to be repeated over Czechoslovakia in 1968). As a consequence, in an example of neo-Stalinisation rather than re-Stalinisation, '1956' hastened the development, and especially the institutional integration within a Soviet-imposed command structure, of the only recently created post-Stalinist Warsaw Pact.

The impact of '1956' upon the society of the Soviet Bloc was, unsurprisingly, a knee-jerk reversion to traditional authoritarian attitudes and policies. Stalinist-style repression to advance social homogenisation became the norm. Cultural conformity through rigorous censorship became the standard objective: Boris Pasternak was forced to refuse the Nobel Prize for Literature awarded for the ambivalent *Dr Zhivago* in 1958 (Keep, 1995). An empire-wide atheistic campaign to peripheralise the role of religion and erode ecclesiastical authority was launched, with Khrushchev personally giving his secular blessing to a state-sponsored crusade against non-Orthodox Christian religions within the Soviet Union (Hosking, 1985). Educational reforms introduced during 1958–9 institutionalised the promotion of Russian over all other languages across the Soviet Union. Pursuing a similar objective, a Sovietisation of the multi-ethnic population of the empire to undermine national identities and therefore weaken national allegiances became fundamental to imperial policy. Khrushchev preached the necessity of immediate *sblizhenie* ('drawing together') of nations to achieve eventual *sliyanie* ('fusion') of nations into a composite Soviet identity (Nahaylo and Swoboda, 1990). Whether interpreted as Sovietisation or Russification, as re-Stalinisation or neo-Stalinisation, the thrust of the social strategy of the post-1956 empire was unmistakable.

Politically, the years after 1956 were notable for a heads-lowered, eyes-downcast torpor throughout the Communist establishments of eastern Europe, which contrasted markedly with the drama of recrimination being played out within the Kremlin. Khrushchev came under heavy and sustained fire from the Soviet establishment over the six months after the 'Hungarian November', accused by Stalinists of bearing the burden of responsibility for the imperial crisis by his intemperate and self-serving campaign of de-Stalinisation. If Hungarians could be partially excused for believing (at least initially) that they were essentially responding to Kremlin promptings during early 1956, then Khrushchev was cast as the scapegoat for the ensuing imperial débâcle.

During early 1957, hardline opponents of Khrushchev led by Malenkov (and subsequently labelled the 'Anti-Party Group') plotted to oust Khrushchev from power. After months of obsessive politicking, an extraordinary plenary meeting of the Central Committee of the CPSU in late June 1957 witnessed a narrow-vote victory for Khrushchev and his allies. A welcome note of de-Stalinisation was struck by the demotion and humiliation rather than the imprisonment or execution meted out by Khrushchev to his defeated rivals (McCauley, 1981; Keep, 1995). 1957 was the year in which Khrushchev survived the Stalinist backlash against his 1956 leadership, though in a fraught and divisive atmosphere of close-won outmanoeuvring rather than ready consensus and traditional triumphalism.

Khrushchev seized every opportunity from mid-1957 to enhance his refurbished but still vulnerable authority. The transition from 1956 had obvious repercussions on the diplomatic scene, with the balmy atmosphere of 'Peaceful Coexistence' reverting to the familiar frostbite of Cold War, particularly after Khrushchev's 'we will bury you' American interview in May 1957. An additional theatre of competition opened when, in October 1957, the Soviet Union launched the first sputnik or artificial satellite. The confrontation between the USA and the Soviet Union instantly assumed a fresh technological dimension in a space race which served the supreme function of defining superpower status. In the short term, the sputnik provided the *coup de théâtre* that the insecure Khrushchev so desperately needed. Having personally patronised the Soviet space programme since 1955, Khrushchev now claimed the political credit for being 'first in space': the Soviet Union may have lagged behind the USA in the atomic race and was still catching up in the arms race, but it had dramatically overtaken the USA in the prestigious space race. In the long term, the effects were very different. Stung into activity by proof positive of its complacency, the USA committed its formidable resources to the space race with a dedication which diverted the Soviet Union, obsessed with maintaining the publicity value of its celebrated breakthrough, away from primary considerations. Serving only to drain indispensable resources from the stretched imperial economy, the space race made a mounting contribution to destabilising an increasingly vulnerable Soviet Empire (Keep, 1995).

In the meantime, however, Khrushchev could bask in the glow of a propaganda triumph which both consolidated his recently challenged leadership and endorsed the viability of the Soviet Empire after the crisis year of 1956. In November 1957, he played flamboyant host to the World Conference of Ruling Communist Parties in Moscow, the first truly international gathering of Communists in power since the dissolution of the Comintern in 1943 (Fejto, 1974). Strutting before an audience which included an unimpressed Mao Tse-tung, Khrushchev set out to flaunt his confirmed political authority within the Soviet Union and to assert his ideological leadership of international communism by redrawing and redefining the Stalinist line after the doubts and disruptions of 1956.

The period immediately following 1956 thereby featured both reaction and readjustment in the Soviet Empire, with an historical record combining instinctive re-Stalinisation and calculating neo-Stalinisation, a return to Stalinist priorities through post-Stalinist techniques and institutions.

What cannot be overlooked is that in one crucial respect the post-1956 Soviet Empire made a fundamental break with its Stalinist past. '1956' effected (or at very least confirmed) a volte-face in the economic strategy of the Soviet Bloc. Until 1953, eastern Europe had been treated as a clutch of colonies for unapologetic imperial exploitation, with its wealth and resources routinely and unceremoniously siphoned east to the Soviet Union. In March 1954, Comecon was assigned the function of permanent economic co-ordinator of the member states of the Soviet Bloc. After 1956, eastern Europe was treated with, to say the least, mounting circumspection (Tampke, 1983; Simons, 1993). Under the terms of its revamped Charter of 1960, Comecon confirmed its change of function from an instrument of imperial exploitation and extortion to an agency of imperial integration and even subsidisation. The flow of wealth which in the Stalinist past had always been from west to east, from periphery to core, was reversed and redistributed to the general advantage of the eastern European colonies.

Soviet imperial strategy in eastern Europe after 1956 bears comparison with that of the USA in western Europe a decade earlier. With ordinary citizens increasingly inclined to articulate their justified grievances, the recently erected but manifestly unstable political superstructure had to be shored up by superpower intervention in the shape of massive financial investment in the economic and social infrastructure. Improving the standard of living of the populace by financial investment and subsidisation was the price that the resident political establishment had to pay to undercut mass popular complaint. Kremlin imperial economic policy after 1956 may therefore be viewed as a belated Soviet equivalent of the Marshall Plan aid denied to eastern Europe by Stalin after 1947.

It comes as no surprise that Hungary furnished the prime example of the economic turnaround in imperial strategy. Military and political repression was predictably tougher in Hungary than anywhere else in eastern Europe. A rolling purge inside and outside the Hungarian Communist party cut a broad swathe through society from late 1956 to June 1958, when Nagy was belatedly executed as a ritual scapegoat for the 1956 débâcle (Morris, 1984). But in order to stabilise the post-1956 Hungarian regime headed by Janos Kadar, universally vilified as a Soviet quisling, the Kremlin felt compelled to grant Hungary exceptionally generous financial treatment. In March 1957, a Soviet–Hungarian economic agreement bestowed special 'favoured status' on Hungary, permitting an astonishing 21 per cent increase in real income for Hungarians over the year 1957 (Okey, 1986). Such 'generosity' had, of course, nothing to do with philanthropy, still less a gesture of apology for the 'Hungarian November'. The objective was to reconcile the most alienated colony in eastern Europe to imperial rule: the bitter pill of national suppression was sweetened by the sugar coating of the most favoured treatment of any east European colony after 1956. Hungary was on the receiving end of the Soviet 'stick' in 1956 but was guaranteed the juiciest 'carrots' from 1957. Hungarians turned out to have lost the battle in 1956 but fortuitously won the war for improved Soviet treatment or, to frame the paradox even more succinctly, Hungary may have 'lost the war but won the peace' (Crampton, 1994: 318).

And yet Hungary after 1956 was exceptional only in the untypical degree of its financial subsidisation. Throughout the Soviet Bloc, the same basic principle of buying off future political trouble by improving material conditions prevailed. Within the Soviet Union, economic decentralisation from Moscow ministries to the smaller union republics, to regions within the larger union republics and especially to new economic councils, was introduced from 1957 to boost production and undercut local and national resentment of the imperial centre (McCauley, 1981). Within eastern Europe, the shift in imperial emphasis from the military stick to the economic carrot was general: the Stalinist exploitation of colonies was halted and replaced by subsidisation geared to preventing a repetition of '1956'.

Hollow Victory

The mid-1950s briefly and tantalisingly raised the possibility of renegotiating Yalta Europe ten years after the end of the Second World War. Over 1954–6, Kremlin initiatives prompted adjustments of jurisdiction which seemed to signal the likelihood of major geopolitical change: within the Soviet Union, Crimea was transferred to the Ukraine as 'a gift from the Russian people' in February 1954; on the frontier of the Soviet Empire, Soviet withdrawal permitted a revived independent state of Austria in May 1955. Despite high hopes, these relatively modest alterations proved to be only the last, delayed episodes in a postwar European settlement which took a full decade to set. After 1956, the postwar settlement congealed in Cold War geopolitical detail, with no external frontier changes to the Soviet Empire until the invasion of Afghanistan in 1979 (and the later débâcle of 1989) and no internal territorial changes of jurisdiction within the Soviet Union until its cataclysmic disintegration in 1991.

The role of Hungary in the process by which the Soviet Empire became, both externally and internally, territorially solidified during 1954–6 was crucial. In attempting to hustle the Kremlin into an act of decolonisation which it perceived as threatening the very existence of the Soviet Empire, Hungary first confirmed the Kremlin in its determination to retain the empire, then guillotined the era of geopolitical renegotation, and finally precipitated a fundamental change in the nature of the continuing empire. Ostensibly, '1956' was an unequivocal imperial victory: the strategic, military, social, political and diplomatic reaction and readjustment after 1956 blended traditional re-Stalinisation with expedient neo-Stalinisation. And yet the imperial victory was seriously qualified: although the Soviet Empire had won the battle in 1956, it was already showing signs of losing the war for ultimate survival. Economically, '1956' constituted an imperial turning-point, a fundamental reversal of Kremlin strategy barely a decade into the existence of the Soviet Empire which amounted to an irreversible act of de-Stalinisation. '1956' brought a characteristically mixed legacy:

63

Yalta Europe would stay for the foreseeable future but, in the interests of geopolitical viability, the post-1956 Soviet Empire would be very different from the exclusively exploitative pre-1956 Stalinist empire.

4

PRAGUE 1968: SPRING
AND FALL

Uncannily repeating the political pattern of the decade of the
1950s, the 1960s and early 1970s witnessed first a climate shift of
'winter into spring', as de-Stalinisation was once again pursued
by the Khrushchev leadership, then a familiar crisis of runaway
de-Stalinisation, on this occasion over Czechoslovakia, and
finally a military-imposed political relapse into an era of reactive
neo-Stalinisation.

Return to De-Stalinisation

The switch from the defensive re-Stalinisation and neo-Stalinisation prompted by '1956' to a renewed campaign for domestic de-
Stalinisation was made public by the XXII Congress of the
CPSU in October 1961. Following a new, orchestrated onslaught
on the reputation of Stalin by congress speakers, a decision was
made to remove the body of Stalin from its joint place of honour
with Lenin in the mausoleum on Moscow's Red Square. The
symbolism of the act for the Soviet Empire entering the 1960s
was unmistakable. For the first time, Stalin was publicly, not just
'secretly' or officially, demoted from the supreme place of honour
in the Soviet pantheon, not that the demotion necessarily meant
disgrace. Stalin's reburial in a plot immediately behind the

mausoleum, still high in the macabre hierarchy of posthumous respect signalled by the gradations of placement between Red Square and the Kremlin wall, did not amount to a comprehensive historical 'un-personing' of the kind that Trotsky had suffered during Stalin's own quarter-century of power (McCauley, 1981). The repositioning of Stalin represented a compromise between the de-Stalinisation course again assumed by the Khrushchev leadership and politick recognition of the Stalinist allegiance of much of both the Soviet *apparat* and the CPSU.

To tackle the very problem of the persistence of Stalinism within the cadres of the Soviet establishment, the XXII Congress introduced a remarkable new constitutional rule. The automatic rotation of office-holders within the CPSU was to be guaranteed by restriction to two, three or four successive terms of service, depending on the hierarchical level within the CPSU (Hosking, 1985). Congresses had not always been convened as regularly as stipulated in party rules (every three years before 1952, every four years thereafter), particularly under Stalin, who appreciated how congresses would have revealed the embarrassing scale of the purges of party personnel over the 1930s and late 1940s. But the new rule, in conjunction with punctiliously regular congresses, meant periodic 'constitutional purges' of the Soviet élite at all levels, designed to prevent extended tenures of power, forestall remote gerontocracies, undermine residual Stalinism and promote new cadres through regular infusions of fresh blood. Proposed by Frol Kozlov, regarded as Khrushchev's designated successor, the 'Kozlov Clause' was intended to encourage an internally less authoritarian, externally more responsive CPSU to emerge from its formative, often traumatic, Stalinist past (Murphy, 1981).

What form should the renewed de-Stalinisation take? Most obviously, the early 1960s returned to the 'thaw' atmosphere of the mid-1950s. The official attitude to culture had always been an accurate barometer of political change in the Soviet Union: not only was the Stalinist insistence on 'Socialist Realism' gradually withdrawn but censorship was increasingly relaxed, especially for works of literature with an explicitly anti-Stalinist message. In autumn 1962, Khrushchev personally cleared the publication of Yevgenii Yevtushenko's warning poem 'Stalin's Heirs' and Alexander Solzhenitsyn's *gulag* (prison-camp) memoir *One Day in the Life of Ivan Denisovich* to signal the permissibility of historical reconsideration and political condemnation of the Stalinist heritage (Keep, 1995).

More fundamentally, the XXII Congress-authorised reburial of Stalin's body was not just an explicit act of de-Stalinisation but, in that Lenin was now restored to sole pride of place in the mausoleum, a tacit act of re-Leninisation. The inspiration for Khrushchev was not the hard-line Lenin of War Communism but the accommodationist Lenin of NEP, with his pragmatic endorsement of a mixed economy and readiness to contract a (temporary) *détente* between socialism and capitalism (Hosking, 1985). In pursuit of Leninist reform, Khrushchev patronised the strategies of economic gurus advocating an orderly retreat from the monolithic Stalinist command economy in favour of a mixed economy and a regulated market.

Within the crucial industrial sector, Professor Yevsei Liberman of the University of Kharkov in the Ukraine publicly advocated from August 1962 a reduction of the jurisdiction of Gosplan, the all-powerful Stalin-created state planning commission. While retaining necessary control of the commanding heights of the economy, specifically the vital coal, steel and armaments industries, Gosplan should withdraw from the consumer industry sector to permit a mutually beneficial direct relationship between producer and consumer (Simons, 1993). Producers should be permitted responsible management with minimal state intervention, and consumers would benefit from improved supply, wider choice and lower prices for goods.

Liberman and his agrarian counterpart, Professor Alexei Zhulin (of the University of Alma Ata in Kazakhstan), advocated producer incentive, profit-related managerial enterprise bonuses and consumer satisfaction at the expense of state monopoly of economic control. Their micro-capitalist strategies found favour with Khrushchev who, following extensive trials and pilot schemes, ordered their implementation across the Soviet Union in the course of the early and mid-1960s (Keep, 1995: 91).

Khrushchev's fundamental motivation in returning to de-Stalinisation was, as ever, pragmatic rather then ideological. Given
the débâcle which resulted from his first de-Stalinisation campaign in the mid-1950s, Khrushchev seems at first sight to have
been either admirably courageous or remarkably foolhardy in
the early 1960s. In reality, the pressures to resume the admittedly
risky option of de-Stalinisation were powerful enough to verge on
the irresistible. Soviet society was straining its Stalinist strait-
jacket, undergoing new processes and expressing fresh demands
which increasingly could not be met by traditional authoritarian
treatment. There was a mounting realisation that both the command economy and the command society inherited from Stalin
must be compromised: the Stalinist reliance on the coercive
'stick' would have to be at least supplemented, if not replaced,
by the Khrushchevite expedient provision of the 'carrot'.

Most pressing of the new post-Stalinist demands on the Soviet
Empire were the space race and the integration of eastern Europe,
both unheard-of expenses ten years before but since 1956 assuming high priority in the newly strained imperial budget. These two
areas of state expenditure, both additional to those engaging the
Stalinist empire, were as pricey as they were novel, requiring the
Soviet economy to increase its productivity to pay for its new
imperial commitments. Economic de-Stalinisation was therefore
a radical, perhaps even desperate stratagem to boost performance
and production in order to cover the growing range of commitments contracted by the post-1956 Soviet Empire.

From Khrushchev to Kosygin

If Khrushchev pursued expedient de-Stalinisation within the
Soviet Bloc over the early 1960s, he indulged in intemperate
neo-Stalinisation towards the wider world. Combining the
supreme offices of First Secretary of the CPSU and Chairman
of the Council of Ministers from March 1958, Khrushchev
demonstrated a new ebullience towards the West, the brunt of
which was borne by the USA. The question of Berlin was

propelled to the top of the international political agenda. As early as November 1958, Khrushchev delivered an ultimatum to the West to withdraw from Berlin within six months (Dunbabin, 1994). Prefaced by the U-2 incident of May 1960, the Berlin Crisis of 1960–1 resulted from the confluence of collapsing East–West relations and a Soviet imperial crisis in the colony of the German Democratic Republic. Suffering from the *Wirtschaftswunder* ('economic miracle') of the German Federal Republic, East Germany had recently experienced an exodus of some two million citizens, an unprecedented brain-drain of professionals which was so damaging to the political credibility and economic viability of the German Democratic Republic that a re-securing of the Soviet imperial frontier was imperative.

If the intrusive and disruptive enclave of West Berlin could not be removed or incorporated without recourse to war, that enclave had to be sealed. In August 1961 a barbed-wire barrier separating East and West Berlin was erected by the security forces of the German Democratic Republic, intended both to exclude Western influence and, primarily, to prevent further leakage of personnel to the West (Roskin, 1994). Thereafter, the 'Berlin Wall' became the ultimate symbol of the Cold War. The West pledged to support front-line West Berlin, most famously in US President John F. Kennedy's declaration that 'Ich bin ein Berliner' in June 1963. The Soviet Empire pledged to establish East Berlin and the German Democratic Republic as the 'shop-window of socialism' against the 'shop-window of capitalism' furnished by the miracle economy of the German Federal Republic.

Most dangerous of all was the Cuban missile crisis of October 1962. The Vienna Summit with Kennedy in June 1961 apparently convinced Khrushchev of a rare opportunity to bamboozle a newly elected, inexperienced and inept American President. Khrushchev accordingly attempted to establish a 'Berlin in the West' by reinforcing Soviet military commitment to Cuba, effectively an eastern enclave in America's Caribbean backyard (Dunbabin, 1994). By raising Cuba from a remote imperial outpost of Soviet influence to a military threat to the mainland of the USA,

Khrushchev may only have been reacting out of frustration over Berlin to improve his strategic position: at the height of the crisis, Khrushchev offered to withdraw all missiles from Cuba if America withdrew all NATO missiles from Turkey, a reciprocal retreat rejected by Kennedy. In the event, while the wider world held its breath, the eyeball-to-eyeball confrontation between Kennedy and Khrushchev over the installation of Soviet missiles in Cuba ended in what was universally viewed as a humiliating climb-down by Khrushchev (Ulam, 1992). At the practical level, the result was for the Soviet Union not so much a retreat as a failure to advance: the USA acknowledged the independence of Castro's Cuba and promised that no American invasion would be undertaken (Ionescu, 1965). At the level of public relations, however, the episode was interpreted as the high point of Kennedy's presidency and statesmanlike leadership of the West against Soviet expansionism.

1962 is generally regarded as the year when the Cold War came closest to becoming hot. Dissatisfaction with Khrushchev among the Soviet establishment had been steadily growing, especially among the CPSU élite thwarted by the 1961 rule restricting tenure of office, and among the *apparatchiks* whose livelihoods and lifestyles were threatened by the new economic reforms (McCauley, 1981). Dismay at the increasingly boorish antics of Khrushchev on the international stage, notably his outrageous shoe-banging performance at the United Nations in September 1960, had already alienated many Soviets from what was regarded as a petulant 'cult of personality'. But it was the Cuban missile crisis which forced general dissatisfaction on into organised conspiracy against Khrushchev. '1962' alarmed the Soviet establishment by its proof of the overwhelming, near-disastrous irresponsibility of Khrushchev in bringing the Soviet Union to the brink of nuclear apocalypse.

The top Kremlin cadres were also dismayed by the breakdown of relations with China. Against a background of deteriorating mutual respect since 1957 caused by Mao Tse-tung's criticism of Khrushchev's ideological revisionism, the Soviet Union revoked its agreement to supply the 'Great Helmsman'

70

of China with atomic bomb expertise in June 1959, damaging Sino–Soviet relations irreparably (Crankshaw, 1984). Over the early 1960s, mutual antagonism reached a pitch which persuaded many observers outside and inside the Kremlin of the likelihood of a Sino–Soviet war (Ulam, 1992). By carelessly antagonising both America and China, thereby raising the perennial Soviet nightmare of a war on two fronts, Khrushchev effectively signed his own death warrant as leader of the Soviet Union (Murphy, 1981).

Khrushchev was neatly, almost surgically, removed from supreme power by a palace revolution in the Kremlin in October 1964. On his return to Moscow after an unwisely timed vacation at a select Black Sea resort, Khrushchev was confronted by plotters within the party presidium, recognised the impossibility of a fight back within the central committee and resigned on the spot (Murphy, 1981). His reward for quitting without fuss was to be pensioned off to live out his seven-year retirement from politics with his family in the peace of a suburban *dacha* (Keep, 1995). In the manner of his going, Khrushchev reaped the benefits of the de-Stalinisation of which he had been the principal (if eccentric) promoter for ten years.

Khrushchev was succeeded by the dual partnership of Alexei Kosygin and Leonid Brezhnev. Like the 'collective leadership' of 1953–5, this partnership was intended to signal a break with the personality cult of their predecessor but again turned out to be an interim arrangement – soon to be attacked by Peking as 'Khrushchevism without Khrushchev' – from which a single dominant personality emerged (Ionescu, 1965: 151). Who that new leader would be was uncertain for a few years after 1964. Comparisons with the last leadership contest during 1953–5 indicated that Brezhnev, as the new First Secretary of the CPSU, filled the winning Khrushchev role, while Kosygin, as a representative of the *apparat*, played the losing Malenkov role. And yet Kosygin appeared to be the senior in the partnership, insisting on an immediate warming of diplomatic relations with the West and a prosecution of economic de-Stalinisation, especially in industry, on a scale which Khrushchev himself had

71

never attempted. To the surprise of many inside and outside the Soviet Union, the coup of October 1964 proved at first an accelerator of, not a brake on, de-Stalinisation. Brezhnev may have made no secret of his reservations about domestic de-Stalinisation but seemed content to play the junior in the partnership for the time being.

Even so, over the later 1960s, the diverging outlooks of Kosygin and Brezhnev made their partnership increasingly strained and their government intolerably schizophrenic. A show trial of the dissidents Andrei Sinyavsky and Yulii Daniel indicated that the emphasis of the partnership was shifting from Kosygin–Brezhnev to Brezhnev–Kosygin, a trend confirmed by the elevation of Brezhnev from a new-style First Secretary to a Stalinist-style General Secretary of the CPSU at the XXIII Congress in March–April 1966 (McCauley, 1981). It was left to a looming imperial crisis in eastern Europe to settle definitively the eventual succession to Khrushchev.

'Socialism with a Human Face'

Eastern Europe in the early 1960s was more content with its treatment within the Soviet Empire than it was prepared to admit openly. The post-1956 imperial shift towards economic cooperation and subsidisation represented a pragmatic deal that most of eastern Europe was prepared to condone: the colonies tacitly deferred ambitions for independence in return for imperial guarantees of a rising standard of living.

What was broadly tolerable in eastern Europe was, of course, viewed less favourably within the Soviet Union. How long was the policy of subsidisation of the colonies, with the Soviet Union picking up the mounting bill for eastern Europe's improving quality of life, intended to last? The Soviet Bloc seemed to be illustrating the world-weary imperial adage that 'colonies start as assets and end up as liabilities'. As re-Stalinisation stabilised eastern Europe and memories of 1956 receded, the Kremlin evaluated imperial subsidisation as a tactical, and therefore temporary, response to an emergency which had clearly passed, and prepared to backtrack. In June 1962, Khrushchev attempted to introduce a new economic strategy of supranational specialisation and integration through Comecon (Ionescu, 1965; Brown, 1991). The pressures for change included the need to match the well-publicised successes of the developing EEC in western Europe, the necessity of boosting productivity to cover the growing range of imperial commitments (most recently, the sponsorship of the German Democratic Republic as the 'shop-window of socialism') and, last but by no means least, the long-term prospect of the impoverishment of the Soviet Union by its imperial responsibilities.

Predictably, eastern Europe, all too soon accustomed to regular and substantial Soviet subsidisation, was reluctant out of economic self-interest to accept any departure from the prevailing bizarre system by which the colonies exploited the imperial centre. On the political level too, eastern Europe resisted any integrating or centralising imperial initiative that might render its eventual independence more difficult to achieve or sustain. While grudgingly but cannily accepting the short-term benefits of forcible membership of what was increasingly described as the 'socialist commonwealth', the colonies of eastern Europe never abandoned hope of their eventual liberation from what they regarded as the Soviet 'prison of nations' (Seton-Watson, 1961).

The state which led and articulated eastern European opposition to Khrushchev's specialisation-and-integration plan was Romania. Over the 1950s, the Communist regime in Romania had been a byword for slavish obedience to the Kremlin. So hardline was Romania towards Hungary in 1956 that, two years later, all Soviet troops were withdrawn from Romanian territory as a gesture of gratitude and an expression of trust. Over the 1960s, however, the increasingly self-confident Romanian leadership became the most recalcitrant Communist renegade in eastern Europe (Tismaneanu, 1992). The Romanian Communist leader Gheorge Gheorgiu-Dej defied Khrushchev's plan to reduce Romania to 'the Kremlin's kitchen-garden', an exclusively agricultural component in an integrated Soviet Empire, instead insisting that Romania develop the full spectrum of its economic potential in the pursuit of eventual self-sufficiency. Backed to a greater or lesser extent by the other regimes of eastern Europe, Romania secured a consensus of defensive self-interest which had by July 1963 scuppered Khrushchev's plans (Tampke, 1983; Swain, 1993). The humiliating failure of Khrushchev to subordinate the colonies of eastern Europe to the priorities of the Soviet Union was a potent extra contributory reason for his removal from power just over a year later.

After Khrushchev's fall, Romania had even greater scope to play the *enfant terrible*. On the death of Gheorgiu-Dej in March 1965, Nicolae Ceausescu succeeded to the Romanian leadership, continuing and developing his predecessor's independent line. Ceausescu pursued a clutch of policies almost gratuitously provocative to Moscow: in May 1966, Comecon was attacked for interference in the economic affairs of Romania; Kremlin plans for greater integration of the Warsaw Pact were blocked; national communism of the most blatant character was officially promoted; and Romania defied the Kremlin line to pursue an independent foreign policy geared to a public courting of the Soviet Union's enemies, most offensively both China and the USA (Brown, 1991).

That Ceausescu could get away with such flamboyant insubordination was attributable to two factors. First, his assertion of an independent line coincided with, and was made possible by, the uneasy and complaisant partnership of Kosygin–Brezhnev in the Kremlin. Secondly, the Romania of Ceausescu presented the Soviet Empire with no problem of law and order: officially a unitary state after the new constitution of 1965, Romania became an increasingly authoritarian regime notorious for repression of the most Stalinist character. Though the gross nepotism of Ceausescu attracted the gibe that the only indisputable achievement of his regime was 'socialism in one family', Romania was too rigorously controlled ever to necessitate military disciplining by the might of the Soviet Empire.

As the 1960s wore on, Romania's fundamental reliability was not matched elsewhere in eastern Europe. Kosygin's patronage of selected economic reforms initiated earlier in the decade by Khrushchev not only affected the Soviet Union but inspired copy-cat reforms through much of eastern Europe. Simultaneously, the forbearance of the Kosygin–Brezhnev partnership towards Romania raised general hopes for a greater Soviet tolerance towards 'different paths to socialism' which might extend to improved prospects for a political federalisation of the Soviet Empire.

Not surprisingly, it was Hungary which pursued what appeared to be the Kremlin-licensed trend most vigorously. Universally vilified as a Kremlin quisling during the late 1950s, the Hungarian Communist leader Kadar redeemed himself in the eyes of most Hungarians over the 1960s by a pragmatic policy of social and economic betterment. In January 1962, Kadar sought to unite Hungarians after the trauma of 1956 with the disingenuous slogan 'those who are not against us are for us', ceremonially amnestying and releasing the imprisoned 'criminals of 1956' in March 1963 (Fejto, 1974). During the mid-1960s, the Khrushchev–Kosygin line was approvingly monitored, then copied by Hungarian government economists, leading to the formal adoption of a mixed-economy strategy under the title of the 'New Economic Mechanism' (or NEM) in January 1968 (Tampke, 1983; Swain, 1993).

·But it was in Czechoslovakia where Kremlin reform was adopted most enthusiastically and where the next crisis of the Soviet Empire was to be played out. Why did Czechoslovakia rather than any other eastern European state prompt this imperial crisis of the 1960s? Almost uniquely among the near nation-states of eastern Europe, Czechoslovakia was fatally riven by a fundamental split between its leading nations, the Czechs and Slovaks. As the new constitution of 1960 provocatively demonstrated, the Communist establishment was dominated by the Czechs, alienating and antagonising the Slovaks. From 1961, a 'Bratislava Spring' among the Slovak intelligentsia generated a more general discontent within Czechoslovakia with the Communist regime headed by Antonin Novotny (Schopflin, 1993). A prison 'trustie' in Mauthausen concentration camp during the

Second World War, Novotny had built two successive careers out of collaboration with occupying foreign powers. The demolition in Prague in 1962 of the largest public statue of Stalin in eastern Europe indicated a widening Czech and Slovak scorn for the colourless old-style Stalinist Novotny and his attempt to promote 'a personality cult without any personality'.

The faltering economic performance of Czechoslovakia was the crucial factor in forcing the Novotny regime into reluctantly following the Khrushchev–Kosygin reforms over the mid-1960s (Swain, 1993). From 1965 (though only formally announced in January 1967), Ota Sik was licensed to introduce reforms on the Soviet model into the stalled Czechoslovak economy (Okey, 1986). Economic de-Stalinisation was soon followed by political and social de-Stalinisation: censorship was reduced, universities were allowed greater freedom, religious restrictions were pruned, greater access to the West was permitted and even decadent rock music was tolerated!

Warned by the East German leader Ulbricht of the dangers of his new line both to Czechoslovakia and its neighbours, and alerted to the growing neo-Stalinist authority of Brezhnev in the Kremlin, Novotny attempted to backtrack on reform in 1967. In a classic demonstration of the mobilising effect of the dashing of raised expectations, Novotny thereby antagonised both the Czech and Slovak intelligentsias, who in June 1967 employed the Writers' Union Congress to censure the government (Zeman, 1969). By October, to the noisy accompaniment of student demonstrations, Novotny and Alexander Dubcek, the reformist leader of the Slovak Communist party since 1963, were locked in a bitter argument over the direction of state policy.

So irreconcilable was the personality clash and policy divergence that a judgement between Novotny and Dubcek had to go to higher appeal (Shawcross, 1970). In December 1967, Brezhnev visited Prague to deliver a Kremlin verdict but, for reasons still unexplained, pointedly declined to endorse the viewpoint of Novotny. This implicit Kremlin no-confidence vote doomed the now-isolated resident leadership: in January 1968, Novotny was replaced by Dubcek as head of the Czechoslovak Communist party (Fejto, 1974). To signal commitment to prudent evolution over precipitate revolution, Novotny was retained as president of Czechoslovakia until replaced on the first day of spring by Ludvik Svoboda, whose surname poignantly and symbolically meant 'freedom'. After the long iron-hard winter of Stalinism, the 'Prague Spring' had at last arrived.

The reformist government led by Dubcek immediately suspended censorship to permit public debate on the future of Czechoslovakia to take place. In April 1968, the incoming establishment published *The Czechoslovak Road to Socialism*, its 'Action Programme' for the implementation of 'socialism with a human face' (Zeman, 1969). The endeavours of the new regime were premised upon neither an Austrian model of negotiated independence nor a Hungarian model of popular defiance but a Yugoslav model of national communism. The monolithic Stalinist command economy was to be revised and adapted in accordance with the Kosygin reforms licensed within the Soviet Union and currently being introduced into Hungary. Meanwhile, the command society was not to be irresponsibly dismantled, indeed the reformist Czechoslovak Communist party was to retain its dominant, if not necessarily its past monopolistic, political status.

The Kremlin was by now concerned at the runaway potential of the Prague Spring, fearing a repetition of 1956. With Prague to the west of such 'Western' cities as Stockholm and Vienna, Czechoslovakia comprised the most westerly salient of the Soviet Empire, enjoyed the highest educational level in eastern Europe and most closely resembled the 'civil society' of the West. After a warning hint from the Warsaw Pact in Dresden in March, Dubcek was summoned to Moscow in May and formally cautioned about the risks he was running. Later in the same month, however, reformists secured the bringing forward of the XIII Congress of the Czechoslovak Communist party to September 1968, a worrying development to the Kremlin. In late June, the Warsaw Pact conducted a major military exercise in Czechoslovakia: Soviet forces were deployed on Czechoslovak soil for the first time since 1945 and, pointedly, were not withdrawn on completion of manoeuvres. Yet within Czechoslovakia, the momentum of change was becoming ungovernable: as the ripples of Western student agitation reached Prague and the reformist liberal Ludvik Vaculik launched his 'Two Thousand Words' appeal to raise the pace of democratisation, Dubcek was conspicuously failing to maintain a firm grip on domestic political developments (Fejto, 1974; Swain, 1993). In July, the Warsaw Pact convened a crisis meeting in Warsaw itself and, when Dubcek declined to attend, baldly demanded the immediate halting and reversal of reform in Czechoslovakia (Narkienciz, 1986).

By this time, the Soviet contingency plan for military intervention in Czechoslovakia had already been finalised. As the only state of eastern Europe to border on both the Soviet Union and West Germany, Czechoslovakia was perceived as a prime conduit for Soviet influence on the West but also as a potential 'dagger aimed at the heart of the Soviet Union'. Whether or not the Kremlin really believed its propaganda about the eastward penetration of disruptive Western pressure, the geopolitical importance of Czechoslovakia to the security of the Soviet Union was indisputable. The impending loss of all control by the Dubcek government and the evaporation of the Communist monopoly of power threatened the Soviet Empire to a degree which dictated a pre-emptive imperial strike into Czechoslovakia.

Only too aware of the hardening attitude of the Warsaw Pact, Dubcek hastened to attend meetings with Brezhnev and Kosygin at Cierna in late July and Bratislava in early August to reassure the Kremlin of Czechoslovakia's unambiguous loyalty to Comecon and the Warsaw Pact (Shawcross, 1970). It was too late: the last straw came in mid-August, when radical new draft statutes compromising the Czechoslovak Communist party's power monopoly were released to facilitate debate and decision at the Party Congress scheduled for the following month. On 20–21 August 1968, in a concerted and intimidatingly efficent military campaign, the armed forces of all members of the Warsaw Pact except Romania invaded and occupied the territory of Czechoslovakia (Ulam, 1992).

To the despair of eastern Europe, recent history had repeated itself all too soon. '1956' and '1968' shared a depressingly similar sequence of events: de-Stalinising reform was initiated by the Soviet imperial centre; the Communist establishments of leading colonies in eastern Europe responded to the Kremlin green light for change; some colonial regimes (like Poland in 1956 and Romania in 1968) contained and channelled their reform drives; other colonial establishments (like Hungary in 1956 and Czechoslovakia in 1968) lost control, eventually attracting military intervention as the alarmed Soviet Empire struck back. Gomulka in 1956 and Ceausescu in 1968, astute and pragmatic party bosses gaining solid advantage from their neighbours' discomfiture, emerged as winners. Nagy in 1956 and Dubcek in 1968, well-meaning but lightweight reformers who were soon out of their political depth and destined to become figureheads and later martyrs for their cause, were indisputably losers (Shawcross, 1970). Paradoxically, the Soviet Union played the twin roles of both promoter and suppressor of de-Stalinisation across its eastern European empire over the 1950s and the 1960s.

Brezhnev and 'Normalisation'

As with '1956', the impact of '1968' reverberated through the Soviet Empire for half a decade. But there were differences as well as similarities between '1956' and '1968', which only gradually became apparent. At the superficial level, '1968' could not be just a repetition or even a reinforcement of '1956'. At a deeper level, differences which emerged over the late 1960s and early 1970s testified to a fundamental weakening of the Soviet Empire beneath its apparent triumph over imperial crisis in 1968.

The political effect of '1968' was predictable. An immediate suspension of de-Stalinisation followed by an authoritative return to re-Stalinisation amounted to 'Neo-Stalinism Triumphant' (Swain, 1993: 159). The supreme casualty in the Kremlin was Kosygin: like Khrushchev after '1956', Kosygin was blamed for causing the runaway crisis in eastern Europe by his disruptive and destabilising reforms. Though retained within the supreme cadre of the Kremlin, Kosygin declined into a spent political force (McCauley, 1981). From late 1968, the Khrushchev–Kosygin economic reforms were officially discredited and soon suffered cancellation across both the Soviet Union and most of eastern Europe.

As the post-1964 Kremlin partnership of equals was dissolved and Kosygin demoted to the level of a sleeping partner, Brezhnev rose to sole supreme power. It was Brezhnev, long dubious about the strategy of subsidising eastern Europe without tangible political return, who articulated the new imperial orthodoxy in an official 'doctrine' which was to be the mission statement of the Soviet Empire throughout the 1970s. Strategically speaking, while Hungary had attempted both defection from communism and independence from the Soviet Empire, Czechoslovakia had modestly attempted only its own style of 'national communism', a distinctively Czechoslovak 'socialism with a human face' within the overall Soviet Bloc. Aware that the Czechoslovak ambitions of 1968 were less flagrant than Hungarian demands in 1956 and therefore the 1956-style crushing of the Prague Spring seemed all the more indefensible, the Kremlin was constrained to produce a general statement of imperial policy.

The 'Brezhnev Doctrine' published in November 1968 reasserted both the geopolitical permanence of the Soviet Bloc and, specifically, Soviet control over the political character of all the Bloc's national components (Tismaneanu, 1992). Ignoring the fact that the Prague Spring had aimed not at the decolonisation of the Soviet Empire but greater autonomy within the Communist bloc, the Brezhnev Doctrine insisted that intervention to maintain the Soviet model of socialism was, and would remain, a legitimate recourse among the 'Communist family of nations'. Such a blatant, almost atavistic return to the Stalinist anti-Titoist tone of the late 1940s embarrassed, offended and alienated large sections of the global socialist movement, which were increasingly disposed to disown the Soviet Empire in the name of 'Eurocommunism' (Narkiewicz, 1986).

Within the Soviet Empire, what was officially (and euphemistically) termed the 'normalisation' of Czechoslovakia proved a protracted and unsatisfactory process. To guarantee its military stranglehold, the Kremlin unilaterally put the temporary presence of Soviet troops in Czechoslovakia, as authorised by a Soviet–Czechoslovak treaty of October 1968, on to a permanent footing in May 1970 (Swain, 1993). In the political sphere, the federalisation of the constitution of Czechoslovakia projected in mid-1968 turned out to be the only reform of the Prague Spring to be permitted by the Soviet leadership, in the cynical calculation that their newfound constitutional equality with the Czechs would convert the Slovaks into supporters of the post-1968 regime.

Despite this Soviet recourse to both 'stick' and 'carrot', the aftermath of the invasion of Czechoslovakia became something of a political shambles. As the later career of Dubcek himself illustrates, the Kremlin experienced problems concocting a subservient replacement regime (Okey, 1986). Unable to recruit a credible Czechoslovak quisling, Moscow permitted Dubcek to retain office for some eight months until April 1969, when Gustav Husak, leader of the Slovak party, assumed the position of First Secretary of the Czechoslovak Communist party. Dubcek was then progressively demoted, exiled by being despatched as ambassador to Turkey in December 1969, then recalled to be expelled from the Communist party in June 1970 (Shawcross, 1970). Almost two years elapsed after the invasion of August 1968 before the 'socialist disciplining' of Czechoslovakia was accomplished through a full-scale purge of all prominent participants in the Prague Spring over the course of 1970 (Swain, 1993). The Czechoslovak Communist party was reduced by one-third as the reformers of 1968 were expelled from power and spitefully allocated the most menial jobs to add public humiliation to their political defeat.

Still, the limitations on Soviet 'normalisation' of Czechoslovakia remained significant. Some 80 000 talented Czechs and Slovaks were lost by political emigration after August 1968. Meanwhile, Dubcek and his fellow reformers retained the high regard of a sympathetic general public. In contrast, Husak never succeeded (unlike Kadar in Hungary after 1956) in swinging a sullenly resentful public opinion round to his own brand of collaborationism, always remaining the despised 'Russian Goose' throughout his eventual twenty-year period of leadership (Glenny, 1990). That Dubcek and the supporters of the Prague Spring were not imprisoned or executed (like Nagy in 1958) may be attributed either to a welcome spirit of humanitarian de-Stalinisation or to Soviet concern not to exacerbate a still dangerously unstable colonial situation by provocative punishment.

Elsewhere across the Soviet Empire, official 'normalisation' was patchily and imperfectly implemented. Within the Soviet Union, the neo-Stalinist clampdown was generally firm though sometimes belated. In 1972, for instance, nine years of cautious de-Stalinisation in the Ukraine came to an end with the replacement of Petro Shelest by the hardline Vladimir Shcherbitsky as head of the Ukrainian Communist party (Murphy, 1981; Keep, 1995). Within eastern Europe, 'normalisation' was typical but not necessarily triumphant or universal. In Hungary, for example, the NEM reforms sanctioned in January 1968 were not abandoned after August. Kadar paid lip-service to Kremlin neo-Stalinisation while covertly maintaining a dogged commitment to the mixed economy, which proverbially converted Hungary from Stalinist 'gulag communism' to entrepreneurial 'goulash communism' over the 1970s. Appreciating that Kadar was surreptitiously continuing de-Stalinisation by stealth, cynics and optimists alike maintained after 1968 that 'the Prague Spring is alive and well and living in Budapest'.

And yet, the impact of '1968' on eastern European society at large was formidable. Many found the climate of reaction and repression which pervaded the Soviet Empire overwhelming. Some individuals despaired of their future and indulged in dramatic acts of moral outrage, like the Czech student Jan Palakh who burned himself to death on Wenceslas Square in Prague in January 1969 to protest at the invasion of Czechoslovakia (Shawcross, 1970). Most people, especially but not exclusively in Czechoslovakia, resigned themselves to mass disillusionment (Glenny, 1990; Tismaneanu, 1992). Previous to 1968, Czechoslovakia had been the most pro-Communist and (next to Bulgaria) the most pro-Russian country in eastern Europe. After 1968, Czechs became among the most anti-Russian and anti-Communist peoples of the Soviet Empire. To so many, '1968' had represented a last spirited initiative to rejuvenate a jaded and compromised Communist movement (Stokes, 1993). The crushing by massive force of an honest attempt at principled reform of communism promoted a pervasive sense of the moral bankruptcy of the Soviet Bloc (Brown, 1991; Ulam, 1992). '1968' effected the mass alienation of eastern Europe: the Soviet Bloc had been exposed as a power-fixated Russian-dominated empire which possessed neither ideological justification nor political legitimacy.

Steady State

Even so, despite the massive damage inflicted by '1968' on its ideological rationale, the Soviet Bloc weathered some five years of imperfectly realised social and political 'normalisation' to claw itself back to an ostensibly healthy and stable condition by the mid-1970s.

The economic impact of '1968' seemed especially salutary for the Empire. If '1956' had prompted a switch in imperial economic strategy from uninhibited exploitation to selective subsidisation of the eastern European colonies, '1968' prompted a turn away from reluctant subsidisation towards more equitable integration. To Brezhnev, the Prague Spring demonstrated the bankruptcy of the post-1956 policy of buying off trouble, which was in any case so draining to the Soviet Union that it could not have been tolerated for much longer even without the imperial crisis of 1968. Much of what Khrushchev had attempted unsuccessfully to foist upon eastern Europe in 1962–3, a shift from subsidisation of the colonies to colonial specialisation within an integrated empire, was imposed by the neo-Stalinist Brezhnev regime in its 'Comprehensive Programme' for economic cooperation approved in 1971 (Brown, 1991).

The effect of this new switch in imperial economic strategy on eastern Europe was undeniably shocking in the short term but apparently beneficial in the medium term. With the knowledge that subsidisation would either cease or (at very least) be significantly reduced, the eastern European establishments found themselves confronted by the unnerving prospect of having to rely much more upon their own economic resources. Regular Soviet subsidisation over the previous decade had rendered the colonies so complacent that a scenario of future collapse of living standards and consequent socio-political upheaval could not be excluded.

The obvious recourse was to find another, surrogate source of external subsidisation. If the East was no longer prepared to underwrite the eastern European economy, then 'the regimes were reduced to the stark choice between stagnation and going West' (Simons, 1993: 155). For capitalism to bankroll communism seemed a preposterous proposition, but the West was currently ready to invest in unconventional medium-risk, medium-profit markets throughout the world. In the course of the early 1970s, the shift in eastern European revenue orientation from East to West was dramatic: all the eastern European states contracted loans on a massive scale from Western banks and governments. The result was not just maintenance but an impressive growth in living standards: Czechoslovakia and Poland, for instance, experienced 40 per cent rises in real wages over the first half of the decade. Although '1968' had effected the bankruptcy of ideological communism, the early 1970s seemed to be demonstrating the viability of the new 'consumer communism' (Brown, 1991; Crampton, 1994: 345).

The effect of the new imperial economic strategy on the Soviet Union appeared to be just as beneficial. Without the subsidisation of eastern Europe, which had weighed like a millstone upon the Soviet economy over the 1960s, the Soviet Union of the 1970s had more money to spend on itself. Moreover, while imperial costs were falling, imperial revenue was rising. For instance, the almost literally rocketing sales of Soviet armaments (including the famous Kalashnikov rifle) to the Third World, particularly Africa and the Middle East, were earning spectacular amounts of hard currency.

Luck too played a part. As its newly extracted Siberian oil came on stream in volume in the early 1970s, the Soviet Union was perfectly placed to exploit the world oil crisis of 1973. The tripling of global fuel prices fortuitously delivered a financial oil bonanza. The Soviet Union could not only sell its oil to the West at an unprecedentedly high price on the international market but, from July 1975, could charge eastern Europe 30 per cent more for its energy supplies in the confident calculation that Western loans would make the extra payment feasible (Narkiewicz, 1986). Thanks to its booming income, the Soviet Union could spare more money for consumer goods, notably in the Five-Year Plan of 1971–5, and displayed its healthiest bank balance in decades (Simons, 1993). Both in eastern Europe and the Soviet Union, the post-1968 strategy seemed to be bringing the Soviet Empire as a whole striking economic dividends and stability.

If the economic position of the Empire dramatically improved in the early 1970s, the enhancement of its military position was still more impressive (Young, 1991). The military resources of the Bloc, already strengthening over the 1960s, received dramatic reinforcement through '1968'. The Cuban missile crisis of 1962 had spotlighted the embarrassing global weakness of the Soviet armed forces, especially in the maritime sphere of operations (Simons, 1993). As a direct consequence, Admiral Sergei Gorshkov secured investment in a massive expansion of the Soviet Navy from its traditional limited function of a 'white-water' coastal defence force to a multi-operational 'blue-water' ocean-going navy (Kennedy, 1988). The creation of a Mediterranean fleet in the mid-1960s and an Indian Ocean fleet in the late 1960s culminated in the deliberately eye-catching 'Okean-75' exercise, intended to demonstrate to the wider world that the Soviet Bloc had by 1975 become a truly global naval superpower.

What the fiasco of '1962' did for the Soviet Navy, the success of '1968' did for the Soviet Army and Air Force. The

overwhelming intervention of the Warsaw Pact in Czechoslovakia, deploying twice the forces employed in Hungary in 1956 and
constituting the largest military operation in eastern Europe since
1945, had been 'a model of its kind', brilliantly organised and
implemented with breathtaking speed and efficiency (McCauley,
1981: 243). Notwithstanding the almost total lack of fighting
resistance to the invasion, the Soviet Army chief, Marshal Andrei
Grechko, played on the crucial dependence of the Brezhnev
Doctrine on military reinforcement. As a consequence, military
funding by, and army authority within, the Kremlin establishment were not merely consolidated but significantly expanded
(Murphy, 1981). In 1972, a joint army and air force exercise
under the codename 'Shield-72' flamboyantly demonstrated the
ability of the Soviet Bloc to defend eastern Europe against
NATO attack.

Such resourceful Soviet economic and military responses to
the crisis of 1968 prepared the way for a striking diplomatic *coup*.
Although the period immediately after 1968 (as after 1956)
experienced a renewed climate of chill in the ongoing Cold
War, the West's genuine sympathy for the 'victims of normalisation' was increasingly overlaid by a grudging respect for the
material achievements of the Brezhnev regime. From as early as
1969, West Germany's Willy Brandt promoted an *Ostpolitik* of
détente with the Soviet Union (Simons, 1993; Dunbabin, 1994).
From 1972, the veteran Soviet foreign minister Andrei Gromyko
entered into active negotiations with the West, employing the
'Shield-72' and 'Okean-75' exercises to pressure the world community in general, and the USA in particular, to come to a
global accommodation. With the recent Soviet achievement of
approximate parity with the USA in nuclear weapon systems, the
time seemed opportune to convene the first full, multipower
conference since 1945.

The thirty-five-nation European Security Conference whose
negotiations concluded in Helsinki in July–August 1975 proved a
diplomatic and strategic triumph for the Soviet Empire. As a
preliminary principle, all signatories accepted and recognised
each other's current territorial jurisdictions. In terms of super-

power relations, American morale had been badly bruised by the shock of President Richard Nixon's forced resignation over the Watergate scandal and the recent débâcle of humiliating withdrawal from Saigon. Represented by the lame-duck presidency of Gerald Ford, the USA was intimidated by the ebullient Soviet Union into renouncing what faint commitment still remained to 'rollback' in eastern Europe (Young, 1991).

By setting the seal on Yalta Europe, 'Helsinki 1975' constituted an act of *détente* between the USA and Soviet Union so fundamental as to cast doubt on the reality of the Cold War. Within months, in December 1975, the so-called 'Sonnenfeldt Doctrine' of complaisant acceptance of the east European *status quo* became the official line of the American State Department (Dunbabin, 1994). The USA's explicit international recognition of the Soviet Empire and its appeasing acceptance of the Brezhnev Doctrine of 'legitimate intervention' have been interpreted as the ultimate sell-out to achieve stand-off, a demonstration of cynical superpower complicity in maintaining a Cold War stalemate (Brown, 1991). A Cold War which had become increasingly unreal since the Cuban missile crisis of 1962 ended in 1975, to be succeeded by a phoney Cold War: after 1975, an essentially 'imaginary war' maintained a charade of confrontation serving the vested interests of both the USA and the Soviet Union (Kaldor, 1990).

In defiance of the flawed achievement of political and social 'normalisation' following the crisis of 1968, 'Helsinki 1975' represented no less than a triumph for the Brezhnev regime, institutionalising diplomatic recognition of the economic and military recovery of the Soviet Union while confirming the renewed domestic and colonial stabilisation together with the new international legitimacy and respectability of the Soviet Empire.

5

GDANSK 1980: STAGNATION TO SOLIDARITY

The decade of the late 1970s and early 1980s witnessed an astonishing reversal of fortunes for the Soviet Empire after its ostensible victory for 'normalisation' was recognised at Helsinki in 1975. The dramatic turnaround had twin, almost equally valid, causes and explanations: first, the triumph of 1975 was superficial to the point of being unreal, masking the deeper problems afflicting the Soviet Bloc; and secondly, the cumulative impact of the internal and international developments of the ten years after 1975 proved devastating to the Soviet Empire.

The domestic counterpart to the Helsinki Accord of 1975 was the new Soviet Constitution of 1977. Tentative discussions at the highest official levels in the mid-1970s had raised the possibility of shifting the Soviet Union further in the direction of supranational socialism, in particular withdrawing the formal right of union republics to secede which was enshrined in the 1924 and 1936 Constitutions (Nahaylo and Swoboda, 1990). But although (or perhaps because) the Soviet Union had been a sham federation for half a century by any Western definition of the term, the final decision in 1977 was to avoid needlessly provoking national sensitivities and to retain the 'paper right' of secession. The Soviet Union was accordingly endorsed as a unitary, multinational federal state with the complacent official slogan 'Socialist in Content, National in Form, Internationalist in Spirit' (Murphy, 1991; Keep, 1995). As with the Helsinki Accord, the 'new' (but actually neo-Stalinist) Third Soviet Constitution affected to celebrate complete recovery after the crisis of 1968 and to set the seal on both the stability and the respectability of the Soviet Empire.

Later hindsight, however, has come to represent the 1977 Brezhnev Constitution as an historic turning-point, the transitory peak of 'high normalisation' on the brink of a new era of what was later to be termed *zastoi*, or 'stagnation'. The Kozlov Clause of 1961, which had attempted to promote regular infusions of fresh personnel into the institutions of the CPSU, had long been a dead letter and was replaced after the XXIII Congress in 1966 by Brezhnev's adoption of the concept of 'confidence in cadres' – to many a cynical gloss on self-serving and self-perpetuating bureaucracy (Hosking, 1985; Keep, 1995). The principle of 'stability of cadres' degenerated through an excess of bureaucratisation into a 'stagnancy of cadres' by the late 1970s. Approaching the 1980s, the Soviet *apparat* featured a bloated personnel establishment and spiralling expenditure without any compensatory improvement in performance. Within the higher Soviet establishment, the Kremlin and CPSU élites became ever more unresponsive, ossified and lazy (Walker, 1993). Taking its cue from the inertia at the top, the lower-level bureaucracy devoted itself to the maintenance of the *status quo*, the protection of privilege and indulgence in the hermetic intricacies of the *nomenklatura* system of patronage and advancement (Schopflin, 1993).

The complacency of the 'administrative-command system' quickly pervaded the economic sector (McAuley, 1992: 75). Buoyed up by the windfalls of the early 1970s, the Soviet economy was allowed to coast. At the command level, 'it was becoming increasingly clear that the Soviet Union and eastern Europe were missing what has been called the second industrial revolution, in which growth depends on the rapid assimilation of information technology' (Simons, 1993: 177). On the shop and factory floor, morale sank to the level of 'they pretend to pay us so we pretend to work' (Hosking, 1991). Pressing economic issues which arose through the 1970s were neglected, shelved or ignored by an establishment which believed its own triumphalist propaganda of successful political and social normalisation and reinforced military and economic stabilisation.

If stagnation marked the political and economic spheres, it was sedation which became the most pronounced feature of society at large. Drink became the favourite recourse (and often the only solace) of a sullen, cynical and alienated population. The consumption of alcohol rose to unprecedented levels over the 1970s, bringing attendant problems of absenteeism from work, industrial accidents, rising crime and marital breakdown; and yet the greater availability of alcohol was still part of a conscious if complacent policy of social control by the establishment. Less dramatically but even more pervasively, state-controlled television was employed as a social sedative: as domestic TV sets became generally available, new viewers were drugged into apathy and hopelessness through the unremitting coverage of a mind-numbing compilation of traditional folk dancing and closely edited spectator sport. Occasional outbursts of dissent from or defiance of the prevailing mood, notably by the cult balladeer Vladimir Vysotsky, only underlined the overwhelming zombieism of the daily life of the Soviet masses by the late 1970s (Keep, 1995).

Having sacrificed its ideological legitimacy in 1968, alienated the bulk of its population by 'normalisation' in the early 1970s and deteriorated during the later 1970s into that most vulnerable of political systems, a command system without commanders, the Soviet Empire was to prove incapable of meeting the burgeoning challenges of the early 1980s.

Empire on the Slide

As the Soviet Bloc drifted almost imperceptibly (to contemporaries) but apparently uncontrollably (in retrospect) from normalisation through stagnation to crisis in the course of the 1970s, it was, predictably enough, the imperial question which seized the early headlines.

The long-term cause of the developing crisis was the prevailing atmosphere of uncertainty throughout eastern Europe about the nature and development of the Soviet Empire. Since the late 1940s, eastern Europe had been militarily and politically dominated by the Soviet Union to the east; but increasingly over the 1970s, eastern Europe became economically orientated towards the capitalist West (Simons, 1993). Although the military and political Iron Curtain rung down in 1948 retained its original location unchanged, the economic Iron Curtain seemed to be shifting eastwards from the established frontier between western Europe and eastern Europe to a new frontier between eastern Europe and the Soviet Union. Since 1956, the economic factor had been undermining the rationale of the Soviet Empire. By the mid-1970s, the situation of eastern Europe could be represented as a form of licensed economic self-determination, raising the possibility that eastern Europeans were already experiencing the first phase in an eventual, full-scale decolonisation of the Soviet Bloc.

The most potent medium-term precipitant of imperial crisis was the emergence of an articulate dissident movement within the Soviet Bloc. The inspiration was Basket Three, Principles 6 and 7 of the Helsinki Accord of 1975, by which signatory states guaranteed observance of basic civil and human rights (Stokes, 1991). Serving as the ambivalent hinge of the 1970s, the Helsinki Accord both sealed the international respectability of the Soviet Empire and inspired a variety of civil rights movements within Communist jurisdiction. The Soviet Union had put its signature to such principles in the (mis)calculation that providing a diplomatic fig-leaf to conceal the discomfiture of the USA in recognising the Soviet Empire involved minimal risk of domestic political resonance (Ulam, 1992). But during the later 1970s, intellectual-led dissident movements mobilised to condemn the prevailing social malaise, protest at arbitrary repression and demand that the Communist establishments observe the international standards of civil rights promised so lightly in 1975 (Brown, 1991).

In eastern Europe, the most respected movement was Charter 77 in Czechoslovakia, led by the playwright Vaclav Havel, which resorted to *samizdat* ('self-publication') to evade state censorship by the private circulation of typewritten political literature (Swain, 1993; Tismaneanu, 1992). Within the Soviet Union, many dissidents clustered around Andrei Sakharov, the prestigious 'father of the Soviet hydrogen bomb', whose principled criticism of the Kremlin establishment won him the Nobel Peace Prize in 1975. Learning from the expulsion of Solzhenitsyn in 1974 that foreign exile only provides a wider platform for dissent, the Kremlin hoped to smother the message of Sakharov by sentencing him to summary internal exile in provincial Gorky in 1980 (Keep, 1995). Encouraged by the Carter administration in the USA, such numerically modest (and sometimes tiny) dissident movements proved disproportionately influential by employing the 'politics of conscience' to embarrass the Communist establishments before both domestic and international audiences (McCauley, 1981).

The short-term trigger to the imperial crisis was indisputably financial insolvency. The prosperity of eastern Europe (and, indirectly, of the Soviet Union too) through the 1970s was artificial and unsustainable. By the end of the decade, eastern Europe owed more both to East and West than it could possibly repay in the foreseeable future. To the East, the world rise in oil prices from 1973 had benefited the Soviet Bloc as a whole, but not eastern Europe, which was compelled to pay the Soviet Union substantially more for its energy and fuel from early 1975 (Morris, 1984; Simons, 1993). Meanwhile, the massive loans contracted by eastern Europe to the West, typically of ten-year duration, were due for repayment by the close of the 1970s. Myopically or wilfully ignorant of the dynamic of capitalism, the eastern European regimes suddenly appreciated the crucial difference between the Soviet subsidies of the 1960s and the capitalist loans of the 1970s (Glenny, 1990). With its 1981 debt to the West fifteen times that of 1970, and with little chance of even servicing the interest on the loans let alone repaying the principal, eastern Europe became part of a global crisis of unredeemable Third World debt (Crampton, 1994: 346). Eastern Europe found itself fiscally trapped between the East (from

1975) and the West (from 1979), an economic double whammy which delivered a financial disaster of unprecedented proportions (Narkiewicz, 1986). Western loans had deferred by a decade a smaller but arguably manageable financial crisis for eastern Europe in the early 1970s at the cost of creating an infinitely greater and probably insurmountable financial crisis for the early 1980s. With the imminent prospect of general bankruptcy throughout eastern Europe, the likelihood of social and political destabilisation was set to rock the Soviet Empire to its very foundations.

Poland's 'Self-Limiting Revolution'

Understudying Hungary in 1956 and Czechoslovakia in 1968, Poland advanced to centre-stage to precipitate the latest dramatic episode of challenge to the Soviet Empire in 1980. Why Poland rather than another country of eastern Europe should be the imperial test-case of the early 1980s rested, as so often, upon a set of independently powerful factors coming together in a new, fortuitously deadly political combination.

At first sight, the obvious question is less why Poland became the *enfant terrible* of the Empire from 1980 than why Poland waited so long to play a role for which history had typecast her. As the largest and most populous state in eastern Europe (outside the Soviet Union itself), Poland always had the geopolitical potential and demographic weight to be the most dangerous troublemaker within the Soviet Empire. Emerging from the Second World War as the most ethnically homogeneous state in eastern Europe, Poland also possessed a spirit of national solidarity unparalleled across the Soviet Bloc. Moreover, the Polish tradition of, indeed almost predilection for, resistance to foreign rule, demonstrated most recently and heroically by the 'Home Army' during the Second World War, could never be safely discounted by the Soviet leadership (Ascherson, 1981). As a direct consequence, Poland was always treated with studied circumspection, if not necessarily respect, by Kremlin authority from its original incorporation within the Empire in the late 1940s up to, and especially during, the imperial crisis years of 1956 and 1968.

But Poland was drawn to assume the troublemaker role for which both history and geography had designed (or condemned) her in the 1970s and beyond. When the government of the increasingly remote and insensitive Gomulka announced price rises in basic commodities just before Christmas 1970, popular demonstrations culminated in a police massacre at the Lenin shipyards in Gdansk (Bethell, 1972). The resulting 'Baltic furore' forced the removal of the veteran Gomulka and his replacement by the more emollient Edvard Gierek, an event which has been described as 'the first occasion in eastern or western Europe since the Second World War when spontaneous actions by workers had dislodged an incumbent ruler' (Crampton, 1994; 360). The episode was loaded with pointers for the future, warning the Kremlin of the Polish potential for challenge, identifying the geographical focus of later popular resistance, stimulating a sense of national martyrdom and moral outrage, and offering a first intimation of the authoritative 'people-power' of the next decade.

A less dramatic but still significant demonstration that the next imperial crisis was likely to be triggered by Poland occurred in June 1976, when another attempt to raise basic prices predictably prompted popular demonstrations on a scale which again forced the government to retreat (Simons, 1993). But not only was the lesson of 1970 reinforced, happily without bloodshed on this occasion, but the popular challenge was becoming more formidable. Workers prosecuted by the government for involvement in demonstrations were supported and defended by KOR, a new organisation formed in September 1976 by the professional intelligentsia for the 'Protection of the Rights of Workers' (Swain, 1993). Whereas previously the workers and the intelligentsia in Poland had discerned no meaningful community of self-interest across the social divide, a rift assiduously cultivated and exploited by the government, from 1976 they began to forge a broad-based coalition promoting a 'civil society' movement against the Communist establishment (Ascherson, 1981; Roskin, 1994).

The stirring of a multiclass opposition coincided with, and was reinforced by, an upsurge in popular Polish nationalism over the late 1970s. The most powerful single stimulus was the election of Cardinal Karol Wojtyla, Archbishop of Cracow, as Pope John Paul II in October 1978. National pride in the first Polish pope was vividly demonstrated during the triumphal papal visit to Poland in June 1979. Congregations of unprecedented size reinforced the independent authority and focus of loyalty of the Roman Catholic Church in Poland (Stokes, 1991). Just as significantly for the future, the vast open-air crowds can be interpreted as the first real demonstration of people-power (Garton Ash, 1990: 133). If 1970 had been the first hint, 1979 was the first manifestation of a people-power which would sweep across the whole of eastern Europe in 1989.

The detonator to crisis in Poland was financial bankruptcy. To buy off social and political discontent, Poland had contracted Western loans on a scale which enabled the raising of average real wages by a spectacular 40 per cent over 1971–5. Unfortunately, the loans were geared to short-term social palliatives rather than long-term economic investment, resulting in increasing shortages after the consumer boom of the early 1970s (Simons, 1993). By 1980, Poland had accumulated the biggest foreign debt in eastern Europe, indeed almost one-half of the total foreign debt of all eastern Europe, forcing the government to attempt an 'austerity package'. Despite its humiliating lack of success in 1970 and 1976, the Gierek government had no recourse but once again to announce price rises in basic commodities in July 1980 (Narkiewicz, 1986; Simons, 1993: 165).

By 1980, however, Polish public opinion was even less disposed to accept the proposed privations than in the past. The dashing in the late 1970s of the raised expectations of the early 1970s lent public grievance an unprecedented militancy. Moreover, the forced revocation of government price rises twice in the last decade engendered a universal confidence that the Gierek government could be faced down once again. The Lenin ship-yard in Gdansk, the now-legendary focus of anti-government protest in 1970, became the cradle of a trade union-based opposition movement called Solidarity, headed by the electrician Lech Walesa (Ascherson, 1981; Stokes, 1991).

From summer 1980 began a trial of strength between the defending Communist establishment and the populist Solidarity. First blood went to Solidarity with the Gdansk Agreement and removal of the discredited Gierek in August–September 1980 (Swain, 1993). As the Warsaw Pact dropped ominous hints about contingency plans for military intervention in Poland, the new premier Stanislaw Kania pursued a determined but pragmatic line against the responsible 'self-limiting revolution' preached by the leaders of Solidarity (Ascherson, 1981). Hopes for a construc-tive and mutually satisfactory accommodation gradually dwindled over the course of 1981. At its IX Congress in July, the Polish Communist party attempted to put its house in better order by agreeing to foster the promotion of lower ranks to effect a more responsive and aware political establishment, a recourse reminiscent of the Soviet Kozlov Clause of 1961 (Simons, 1991). In September, the belated First Congress of Solidarity convening in Gdansk displayed a radical, assertive and uncompromising face which confirmed an unbridgeable polarisation between the Communist establishment and dissident (or at least unofficial) Polish society (Crampton, 1994).

In October, Kania conceded the bankruptcy of his strategy of negotiated compromise by resigning office. He was succeeded by the new strong man of Poland, Marshal Wojciech Jaruzelski: first Minister of Defence and then Premier, Jaruzelski now added the post of First Secretary of the Polish Communist party to his portfolio of supreme power. In December 1981, Jaruzelski employed his unprecedented concentration of governmental authority to arrest the leaders of Solidarity and impose martial law across Poland (Garton Ash, 1983; Swain, 1993). The Com-munist establishment in Poland had determined to resolve the lingering crisis: 'Gdansk 1980' was countered by 'Warsaw 1981'.

1980, 1968 and 1956

In comparing the turning-points in the career of Communist eastern Europe, it is the striking dissimilarities between Poland in 1980–1 and the earlier imperial crises in Czechoslovakia in 1968 and Hungary in 1956 which are the most revealing about the declining fortunes of the Soviet Empire.

In the first place, the Polish crisis of 1980–1 was not a reactive colonial response to a Kremlin reform initiative, as in the early stages of the movements in Hungary in 1956 and Czechoslovakia in 1968. The Polish movement developed its own momentum over the 1970s independently of the actions (or rather inactions) of the leadership of the Soviet Empire. In 1980, Solidarity burst into public life in protest at both the perceived mismanagement of the Gierek government and the stagnancy and inertia of the Kremlin leadership. What was later to proclaim itself a 'self-limiting revolution' was also an essentially self-starting revolution, providing its own essential dynamism rather than responding opportunistically to Kremlin reform like its predecessors in 1968 and 1956.

Secondly, although the Polish movement was suppressed by military force, the expected external intervention by the Warsaw Pact never materialised. Under the explicit threat of such an invasion, Jaruzelski employed the Polish army to crack down on Poland in December 1981, lifting the threat of Warsaw Pact action at the expense of widespread vilification as a Polish quisling doing the dirty work of the Kremlin (Dunbabin, 1994). Whether this recourse was preferable to foreign suppression naturally became the prime talking-point within Poland. To some, Jaruzelski was a traitor to Poland who had sold out to the Russians, assigning to Polish soldiers the disgraceful and ignominious role of oppressors of their own countrymen. To others, Jaruzelski represented the lesser of two evils, saving Poland from foreign invasion and retaining for Polish society substantially more freedom than would have been possible under a Soviet occupation (Roskin, 1994). If suppression was unavoidable, there were clear advantages to suppression by 'Warsaw without the Warsaw Pact'.

The next question follows naturally: why was Poland spared the external military intervention which so definitively terminated similar developments in Hungary in 1956 and Czechoslovakia in 1968? One plausible argument emphasises the individuality, even uniqueness, of Poland's internal position within the Soviet Empire. As the largest state of eastern Europe, Poland was a much more formidable proposition than Hungary, the smallest of the eastern European colonies. Poland was also ethnically almost homogeneous and featured a glorious tradition of nationalist military resistance, in marked contrast to nationally divided and traditionally unheroic Czechoslovakia. As a consequence, the Kremlin was less inclined to risk an interventionist military solution in Poland than anywhere else in eastern Europe.

An alternative interpretation stresses the external pressure applied by the USA to prevent Soviet intervention. With the Polish–American lobby stronger than any other eastern European voice in Washington, the USA maintained a greater protective interest in Poland than in either Hungary or Czechoslovakia. The Carter administration had already flexed its muscles by suspending vital wheat exports to the Soviet Union in 1980 in protest at the invasion of Afghanistan. Although the incoming Reagan administration raised the embargo, the American economic threat to the Soviet Union had never seemed more real (Dunbabin, 1994). As a consequence, whereas the USA did little but make disapproving noises and – for shame – admit political refugees in 1956 and 1968, it adopted a harder stance in 1980–1 which may have tipped the balance against Soviet intervention in Poland.

Another line of explanation, expressed simplistically, suggests that Afghanistan saved Poland. The ill-advised Soviet incursion into Afghanistan in December 1979 deployed military personnel and material on a scale which precluded a similar intervention in Poland (Crankshaw, 1984). More generally, its traditional strategic fear of a war on two fronts made the Soviet establishment reluctant to invest simultaneously in Afghan–Asian and Polish–European operations. Moreover, as the Soviet Army was drawn inexorably further into Afghanistan, the prospect of a Soviet

Vietnam further undermined confidence in the success of an invasion solution for Poland. It is likely that the Polish argument, the American argument and the Afghan argument were complementary rather than mutually exclusive, together persuading the Kremlin to accept, albeit grudgingly, the local solution embodied in the martial law regime of Jaruzelski.

A final difference between 1980–1 and the earlier imperial crises was the manifest absence of a clearcut resolution to the Polish confrontation. Though the Soviet responses both to Hungary in 1956 and Czechoslovakia in 1968 were in reality less overwhelming than first appears, the ongoing crisis in Poland after 1980 was remarkable for its lack of denouement. Although the leaders of Solidarity were arrested in December 1981 and Solidarity itself was formally banned by the Polish *Sejm* (Parliament) in October 1982, the movement maintained a political existence and social presence. The underground *Konspira* organisation was particularly successful in keeping the fighting spirit of Solidarity alive. On the government side, the martial law imposed in December 1981 was suspended as early as December 1982 and formally lifted in July 1983 (Swain, 1993; Stokes, 1993). The early and mid-1980s witnessed less a victory for the Communist establishment over popular opposition in Poland than a stand-off between opposing camps of comparable political weight and resources.

The forcible suppression by the military in Poland of the mass of the workers, in whose name Communism claimed to operate, reinforced that universal sense of the moral bankruptcy of the eastern European establishments which had prevailed since 1968 (Tismaneanu, 1992). At the same time, the surprising non-intervention of the Warsaw Pact in Poland raised hopes that the military resources of the Soviet Empire were overstretched, fostering the sense of a widespread, unresolved and (very possibly) unresolvable crisis across the eastern Europe of the 1980s. The Soviet Empire seemed to have run out of options: the exploitation and extortion of the period 1948 to 1956 had been succeeded by subsidisation and specialisation from 1957 to 1968 and subsequently by disengagement and detachment following

1969. Each imperial option failed in turn, precipitating the almost rhythmic sequence of crises of 1956, 1968 and 1980. Each imperial crisis prompted another increasingly desperate switch in financial strategy towards the colonies of eastern Europe.

Moreover, each episode proved more resistant to satisfactory resolution than its predecessor, fostering the distinct impression that current and future crises could no longer be permanently solved, only temporarily managed. As the Soviet Empire was increasingly diagnosed as the 'Sick Man of Eurasia', the medical prescription settled for courses of treatment rather than entertaining hopes of a permanent cure. Along with the ongoing Polish confrontation surfaced the almost unthinkable realisation that, by a process of elimination, since all available imperial options had already been tried and failed, only the ultimate option remained for the late 1980s: the decolonisation of the Soviet Empire.

Empire in the Red

Running parallel to the resurgent imperial crisis was a linked but essentially discrete and novel crisis in the economic health of the Soviet Bloc which also came to a head during the early 1980s.

The income of the Soviet Empire declined precipitately between the early 1970s and early 1980s. Oil prices on the international market collapsed from $35 to $16 a barrel in the first half of the 1980s, preventing a repetition of the financial killing made from capitalism a decade earlier (Walker, 1994: 328). But even if world prices had been high, the Soviet Bloc was no longer in a position to exploit the international market. Soviet oil production, always technically wasteful and environmentally damaging, decreased from the early 1980s as readily accessible sources of crude oil were exhausted. Although massive deposits of oil and gas had been prospected in deepest Siberia, the climatic and logistical obstacles to extraction were insuperable without the most sophisticated (that is to say Western) technology (Keep, 1995). This equipment was too expensive for the limited hard-currency resources of the Soviet Union to buy in, even if the USA of Ronald Reagan had been prepared to allow such technology transfer to its sworn enemy (Glenny, 1990). Neither could the 'captive market' of colonial eastern Europe be charged extra for its dependence on Soviet-supplied energy: by the early 1980s, the dire financial straits of eastern Europe precluded any fresh strategy of extortion to redress the economic shortfall caused by the Soviet dip in domestic oil and gas production. The Soviet Empire's windfall oil bonanza of the early 1970s had entirely evaporated a decade later.

Even more disastrously, while income was significantly down, expenditure was dramatically up. In the first place, like Hungary in 1956 and Czechoslovakia in 1968, Poland in 1980–1 also prompted a fundamental change in imperial economic strategy. After turning a financial cold shoulder to eastern Europe over the 1970s, the Soviet Empire was confronted with the bankruptcy of Poland and all its neighbours, necessitating a return to subsidisation, albeit limited and selective. Financial rescue packages for the eastern European colonies were brokered by the Kremlin, which typically guaranteed to service the interest (but not the capital) on Western loans. During 1981–2, Poland and then Romania negotiated reschedulings (that is to say, postponement) of foreign debt repayment, underwritten by the Soviet Union in return for the implementation of cost-cutting austerity packages (Simons, 1993; Stokes, 1993). The eastern European financial millstone, temporarily removed from around Soviet necks over the 1970s, weighed even more when it was restored over the 1980s.

A clutch of new demands on the imperial budget characterised the early 1980s. The Soviet intervention in Afghanistan demonstrated the almost prohibitive costliness of modern war. In the light of the recent American experience in Vietnam, it was testimony to the degenerating leadership of Brezhnev (who had raised himself to the rank of Marshal of the Soviet Union in 1976) that such an ill-judged incursion should be considered, let alone implemented (Hosking, 1985). As the short-term decisive campaign envisaged in December 1979 became a war of attrition dragging on more than twice as long as the Second World War, the various political, diplomatic and financial costs of the Soviet Vietnam spiralled. Once the fatal decision to intervene was effected, the Soviet Empire was drawn inexorably by 'mission creep' into a financial black hole from which no practical military escape, honourable diplomatic extrication or solid political advantage seemed possible.

Another costly exercise was the Moscow Olympics of summer 1980. Predictably enough, the motive for the Soviet Union's successful bid to host the Olympics for the first time was less about applauding sporting excellence than parading imperial triumphalism. The XXII Olympics were to be hijacked to serve as the culminating extravaganza in a trio of events advertising the stability and respectability of the Soviet Bloc: after the Helsinki Accord of 1975 and the Soviet Constitution of 1977, the Moscow Olympics were to celebrate Brezhnev's grandiose vision of the Soviet Empire. The projected Soviet showpiece was, of course, spoiled by an American-led sixty-two nation boycott of the Olympics in protest at the invasion of Afghanistan (Roskin, 1994). The 1980 Olympics became an embarrassment to the international Olympic movement while the intended Soviet self-glorification before a global audience misfired, with damaging diplomatic and grievous economic repercussions.

Finally came the financially apocalyptic prospect of 'Star Wars'. Following his denunciation of the 'Evil Empire' in February 1983, American President Ronald Reagan terminated the tacit superpower phoney war which had prevailed through most of the 1970s to pursue a new or second Cold War against the ailing Soviet Bloc. Appreciating Soviet respect for American technological superiority, Reagan announced in March 1983 the Strategic Defense Initiative (SDI), a space-based deployment of 'smart' laser weaponry, which would effectively convert the peacetime space race of the previous quarter-century into a future Armageddon of the superpowers (Dunbabin, 1994). Whether the grandiose strategy of SDI was science fiction masquerading as science fact, a supreme piece of American disinformation and bluff, remains a matter of continuing controversy (Kennedy, 1988).

By contrast, the intimidating and ultimately disabling impact made by the challenge of SDI on the Kremlin was incontrovertible. Either by accident or design, Reagan was upping the strategic stakes precisely at a juncture when much of the Soviet military equipment (most notably in the Soviet Navy) was approaching 'block obsolescence' after the expansion period of the late 1960s and early 1970s (Kennedy, 1988). The financial cost of replacement alone bordered on the prohibitive, with the military demands of superpower status draining away the dwindling resources of an overextended Soviet Empire on the brink of bankruptcy (Fernandez-Armesto, 1995). Whether even the USA could have realised or afforded SDI still remains in doubt. What is certain is that the Soviet Bloc had neither the military capability, the technological skills nor the financial resources to counter SDI, a realisation which delivered a devastating body-blow to the collective morale of the Soviet political and military establishment.

By the mid-1980s, the Soviet Empire was not only incapable of rising to the challenge of a crop of new major items of expenditure but was demonstrably failing to maintain existing services and standards. The austerity packages introduced across eastern Europe at Soviet insistence in the early 1980s put a stop to the steadily rising standards of living which had become taken for granted through the 1970s. With the dashing in the 1980s of the legitimate expectations of the 1970s, economic-based discontent grew. The Hungarians, for example, complained at having to pay 'Swiss taxes on Ethiopian wages' (Crampton, 1994: 409). That so pungent a comment could be couched in such terms was itself indicative of growing eastern European awareness of their relative deprivation by comparison with the West, a street-wise worldliness born of increasing foreign travel and exposure to Western media and tourism.

The 'new deprivation' was manifestly not just relative but absolute. During the early 1980s, the financial plight of the Soviet Bloc, exacerbated by a run of bad harvests caused by drought, forced a general reduction in state welfare – as evidenced by rising infant mortality and declining adult life expectancy – precipitating an undeniable decline in the quality of life of the average citizen (Kennedy, 1988; Keep, 1995). 'Consumer communism', the ideologically embarrassing economic hybrid which had extended the life of communism over the 1970s, was conspicuously failing to deliver in the 1980s. As with the imperial dimension, so with the often undervalued but crucial economic dimension, the slide in the prospects of the Soviet Bloc was rapid and remorseless. The 'Lucky Seventies' became the 'Bankrupt Eighties' for the stricken Soviet Empire.

Grey Eminences

The growing number and critical nature of the challenges confronting the Soviet Empire coincided with (and to a significant extent were a product of) an ageing, then a senile and ultimately a moribund Kremlin personnel establishment. Starting with the death of Tito in Yugoslavia in May 1980, the half-decade of the early 1980s cut a brutal swathe through the older generation of leadership across much of the Communist Bloc.

As personified by Brezhnev, the Kremlin establishment of the early 1980s was universally perceived as a gerontocracy of Old Stalinists guarding their own coffins, insulated from reality and both unwilling to contemplate and incapable of undertaking a constructive response to accelerating change. Although accumulating almost unprecedented formal power, becoming President of the Soviet Union as well as General Secretary of the CPSU in 1977, Brezhnev (and his sycophantic cult of personality) symbolised the degeneration of the neo-Stalinist regime. Physically ailing but sustained by artificial means, managerially incompetent but retained as a figurehead of the neo-Stalinist generation, Brezhnev became the personal embodiment of stagnation and sedation (Murphy, 1981; Keep, 1995). Permanently drugged, often uncomprehending and increasingly unpresentable in public, Brezhnev represented a Soviet generational establishment which was tolerated largely because its biological and therefore political life-term was so obviously almost up.

On the death of Brezhnev at the age of seventy-six in November 1982, Yurii Andropov became the new leader of the Soviet Union. Although taking modest executive initiatives, notably a campaign to combat alcoholism, Andropov confirmed his reputation as an unreconstructed neo-Stalinist. The efforts of the man who, as Soviet ambassador to Hungary in 1956, had 'called in the Russians' and later headed the KGB from 1967 to 1982, were now geared not to fundamental reform but to improving efficiency by combating corruption within the existing structure (Hosking, 1985). Moreover, Andropov was convinced of the aggressive intentions of a future SDI-armed America. Although the degree of his personal responsibility in the affair remains unclear, Andropov's fourteen months in supreme office were dominated by the Soviet downing of civilian airliner KAL007 in Soviet airspace over Kamchatka in September 1983. The death of 269 innocent passengers and crew chilled the new Cold War a few more degrees and confirmed Ronald Reagan in his hardline strategy against the recently denounced 'Evil Empire' (Dunbabin, 1994).

The death of the seventy-year-old Andropov in February 1984 brought the seventy-three-year-old Konstantin Chernenko to the leadership (Keep, 1995). As, to quote the contemptuous contemporary Soviet comment, 'the half-alive was succeeded by the half-dead', the neo-Stalinist élite reached its final, ignominious political throw. Knocking at death's door throughout his thirteen-month nominal leadership, Chernenko carried no qualifications for political eminence other than 'greyness', his undistinguished membership of the numerically dwindling colourless élite of neo-Stalinist geriatrics.

The sheer frequency of succession crises in the Kremlin in the early 1980s, three inside three years, demonstrated how the Stalinist Old Guard of living political fossils was inexorably dying off. The unconscionably long-lived generation of neo-Stalinist dinosaurs was finally becoming extinct and would have to be replaced by a fresh, essentially post-Stalinist generation at every level of the Soviet establishment. With the unmourned death of Chernenko in March 1985, the way was at last clear for a new Soviet leadership to tackle the long-deferred but now unpostponable political, economic and social crises confronting the ailing Soviet Empire.

6

BERLIN 1989:
DECOLONISATION
OF THE OUTER EMPIRE

The ten-year decline of the Soviet Empire preceding 1985 was succeeded by an increasingly precipitous fall, which effected first the decolonisation of the outer empire of eastern Europe and then the disintegration of the inner empire of the Soviet Union. As so often with empires in supreme crisis, the final downfall of the Soviet Bloc was the product of both a push-out of colonial liberation and a pull-out of imperial withdrawal, a complex blend of self-serving, even mutually advantageous colonial and imperial self-emancipation.

Gorbachev and *Glasnost*

The new General Secretary of the CPSU appointed on 11 March 1985 was the fifty-four-year-old Mikhail Gorbachev. A candidate member of the Politburo since 1979, Gorbachev was nearly elevated to supreme office on the death of his patron Andropov in February 1984 but was then denied his final promotion to serve another year as heir-apparent under the caretaker leadership of Chernenko (Hosking, 1991). Although much has been made of his youth, Gorbachev was not in Soviet terms especially young for supreme office: Brezhnev was fifty-eight on appointment as First Secretary of the CPSU in 1964; Stalin was forty-nine on assuming the Soviet leadership in 1928; and Lenin was only fifty-three when he died in 1924!

The key point was that Gorbachev represented a previously promotion-blocked younger generation in their forties and fifties replacing the outgoing élite in their sixties and seventies. To quote a contemporary Soviet joke: 'Is Gorbachev supported in the Kremlin? No, he can walk unaided' (Walker, 1993: 73). This new generation was essentially post-Stalinist: Gorbachev was twenty-two at Stalin's death, so his Stalinist childhood and youth was followed by a post-Stalinist adulthood. Gorbachev also represented an alternative style of politician: the first leader of the Soviet Union to be a university graduate (in law and then economics), he was a professional by inclination and training, not just a functionary elevated through blind obedience to the CPSU (Hosking, 1991). Little wonder that contemporaries saw in the promotion of Gorbachev a watershed in the development of the political leadership of the Soviet Empire.

The pre-1985 legacy inherited by Gorbachev was, however, daunting in the extreme. In imperial terms, the long-term campaign to replace national ethnic identity with supranational socialist allegiance had demonstrably failed across eastern Europe and stalled across the Soviet Union. Since its hurried creation in the late 1940s, the Soviet Empire had defied a variety of Kremlin strategies, eventually exhausting all available imperial economic options. Morale within the 'restless empire' was at its lowest historical ebb, with negligible ideological commitment among the rulers and universal disillusionment among the ruled (Keep, 1995: 307). Economically, the Soviet Empire was on the brink of bankruptcy, with expenditure rocketing but income falling. Among the first reports to land on the new leader's desk were a gloomy confirmation that societal stagnation had undermined the superpower status of the Soviet Empire and a pessimistic forecast that by 1988 the gross national product of the Soviet Union would drop to fourth place in the world, behind not only the USA but also West Germany and Japan. It was all too obvious to the incoming Gorbachev that vigorous measures were necessary to tackle the heavy burden of the past.

Gorbachev's initial reforms were conducted under the *uskorenie* (or 'acceleration') slogan. The concept of acceleration was intended to convey official confidence that the fundamental mechanism of the Soviet Union was sound, requiring only a thorough seventy-year service and fine tuning by dedicated engineers to regain its exemplary past performance. Such a conventional gloss may also suggest that Gorbachev was still unaware of the scale of the crisis he was expected to resolve. Essentially a continuation of the policy of his mentor Andropov, 'acceleration' testified to the relative modesty of Gorbachev's early domestic initiatives (Tismaneanu, 1992; Walker, 1993).

Infinitely more eye-catching was Gorbachev's performance on the international stage, introducing the observation that he was always to be more popular and successful abroad than at home. Whereas Andropov had been alarmed by SDI into open hostility towards the USA, Gorbachev recognised that SDI necessitated expedient *rapprochement* with the West. With defence spending variously calculated as accounting for between 16 per cent and 28 per cent of the Soviet budget, a proportion which could not be increased even to counter SDI, Gorbachev chose to opt out of the new Cold War of superpower confrontation (Roskin, 1994: 134). With so many other financial demands upon the imperial budget, only the military account was substantial enough to have the potential for meaningful redistribution to other, conspicuously underfunded sectors of the economy. By coming to an accommodation with the USA, Gorbachev planned to prune defence spending and invest the savings of the 'peace dividend' in tackling the glaring deficiencies in the economy and society of the Soviet Union (Walker, 1993).

The new diplomacy was signalled by Gorbachev's replacement of the veteran Andrei Gromyko ('Grim Grom') as foreign minister by the almost unknown Eduard Shevarnadze in July 1985. Within months, the telegenic Gorbachev was conducting his personal 'charm offensive' in the West, making overtures to President Mitterrand of France on his first foreign trip as Soviet leader in October 1985 and floating the possibility of arms control to President Reagan at Geneva a month later. By the time of the Reykjavik Summit in October 1986, Gorbachev had earned (or at least attracted) the unstinting approval of the West by agreeing to the principles of arms limitation with the USA and Soviet military withdrawal from Afghanistan, both eventually realised in the course of 1988 (Wright, 1989).

But success abroad only threw into greater relief the limitations and inadequacies of 'acceleration' at home. For example, a well-meaning but ill-conceived anti-alcohol campaign backfired disastrously. Wine-producing areas were devastated, fomenting a wave of anti-Russian feeling across the southern Soviet Union. Illicit moonshine replaced unavailable proprietary alcohol, with dire medical and social effects nationwide. State revenue dipped by 6 per cent, exacerbating the imperial budget crisis. As the perpetrator of prohibition, Gorbachev alienated wide sectors of the Soviet populace (Walker, 1993; Keep, 1995). Far from popularising acceleration, the prohibition campaign effected deceleration in both economy and society.

Buoyed up by diplomatic progress and now better informed of the urgency of domestic problems, Gorbachev welcomed 1986 by abandoning acceleration in favour of a new watchword: *glasnost* or 'openness'. Perhaps overreacting to his popularity abroad, Gorbachev gambled on establishing a greater measure of social consensus in future political decision-making within the Soviet Union. As formally approved by the XXVII Congress of the CPSU in February 1986, *glasnost* permitted, indeed encouraged, the politics of public concern. The political, economic and social repercussions of past 'stagnation', in part the product of the closed CPSU decision-making procedures symptomatic of the Brezhnev era, could only be remedied by recognising and confronting the issues in public (Wright, 1989; McAuley, 1992). As, from spring 1986, state censorship was progressively relaxed, first in the press and soon afterwards in radio and television, and a fresh officially sponsored climate of thaw pervaded the Soviet Union.

With initiatives on the diplomatic, political and social fronts all bearing fruit, Gorbachev turned to the vexed economic dimension. Government moves throughout late 1985 and 1986 indicated that Gorbachev was venturing beyond mere overhaul to radical redesign: a break from monopolistic state control and a return to the mixed economy was becoming the new orthodoxy (Hosking, 1991). Citing legitimising precedents before and after the Stalinist era, from Lenin's NEP in the 1920s to the reforms of Khrushchev and Kosygin in the 1960s, Gorbachev unveiled the new (or revamped) policy of *perestroika* (McAuley, 1992). In explicitly promoting a mixed economy blending socialism and capitalism, an option which had been summarily dismissed for twenty neo-Stalinist years, and implicitly permitting a pluralistic societal infrastructure, 'reconstruction' or 'transformation' emphasised the primacy of Western-style pragmatism over Soviet-hallowed dogma.

The dual principles of *glasnost* and *perestroika* authorised by Gorbachev in 1986–7 together amounted to commitment to a third de-Stalinisation campaign. After the unsuccessful first campaign of 1955–6 and second campaign of 1961–8, which now earned Khrushchev a posthumous reputation as the 'grandfather of *perestroika*', the Stalinist establishment in the 1980s appeared sufficiently weakened for a third campaign under Gorbachev to make a long-deferred but definitive break with the lingering legacy of a tyrant who had died one-third of a century before.

This is not to suggest that Gorbachev was a reforming liberal, though the image was cultivated by an adoring international claque enthused by uncritical Gorbymania. As with Khrushchev, Gorbachev was never a liberal in any Western sense of the term, still less a genuine convert to people-power (Keep, 1995). True to the Communist upbringing which eventually brought him to supreme power, Gorbachev responded to the multifaceted crisis of the Soviet Bloc by resorting to whatever state-controlled, CPSU-sanctioned reform was necessary to restore the fortunes of the Soviet Empire (Walker, 1993). Gorbachev was not personally committed to any Western-style liberalisation or democratisation of politics and society. Revolutionary only in the sense that

Ivan the Terrible, Peter the Great, Alexander II and Stalin himself had been 'within-system radicals', Gorbachev was a 'revisionist tsar' set on preserving the traditional Russian autocratic monopoly of 'revolution only from above'.

The Impotence of the Powerful

Although desperate situations demand desperate remedies, there was never any gainsaying the high element of risk in Gorbachev's reform strategy. Separately, *glasnost* and *perestroika* were each inherently destabilising programmes of reform. Together, *glasnost* and *perestroika* constituted a mutually reinforcing combination with almost infinitely dangerous potential for disrupting the Soviet Empire.

Within months of the official announcement of *glasnost*, the mass media were shelving both the externally imposed and self-regulatory censorship of the past and taking the lead in responding to, and often racing far ahead of, declared government policy (Remnick, 1994). The revolution in the media, which was to gather eventually unstoppable momentum, raises the question of why Gorbachev embarked upon such a risky policy.

Ostensibly at least, such concessions as the phased unjamming of the BBC Russian Service from January 1987, the BBC World Service from January 1988 and Radio Liberty and Radio Free Europe from December 1988 constituted a conscious and deliberate policy voluntarily undertaken by state authority in a spirit of the responsible prosecution of necessary reform.

In reality, Gorbachev was only bowing to the inevitable and hoping to make a virtue of necessity. The revolution in information technology had made such inroads into even the protectionist Soviet Union by the mid-1980s that a reformer had no option but to 'license the unavoidable' by sanctioning *glasnost*. Continent-wide telephoning and (later) faxing made effective supervision impossible. The mass influx of cheap videos (a major element in the Iranian Revolution of 1979) could not be stemmed, still less prevented. The growing availability of typewriters and tape-recorders, then photocopiers (against which the KGB had battled for years) and finally word-processors made alternative information dissemination unstoppable. The collective impact of the 1980s' revolution in media technology made the traditional Soviet insistence on its hermetic monopoly of news through the exercise of information suppression and diffusion problematic to the point of being almost quaintly anachronistic.

The news breakthrough which followed the adoption of *glasnost* was publicised by a run of often sensational exposés, without exception to the detriment of the Soviet establishment. The fundamental failure of Soviet government to provide adequately for the welfare of its citizens was the first to be exposed to public gaze. Press allegations that the scandalously under-resourced health service was collapsing to the level of a Third World country shocked, but did not surprise, the general populace (Keep, 1995). An earthquake which destroyed Spitak and Leninakan in December 1988 but would in the pre-*glasnost* past have been dismissed as a natural disaster (or even as an act of God by the local Armenians) was now portrayed by the more daring of the mass media as a predominantly man-made catastrophe. Responsibility for most of the 30 000 casualties which resulted from the worst earthquake in Soviet history was put down to the appalling design, construction and maintenance of local housing (Wright, 1989).

Failure and incompetence in the Soviet armed forces, traditionally the pride of the Soviet populace, was also subjected to the full glare of unwelcome publicity. The war in Afghanistan continued to drag on through the 1980s, a painful if non-life-threatening 'bleeding wound' (in Gorbachev's 1985 phrase) afflicting Soviet society (Wright, 1989: 89). From the moment of intervention in December 1979, the war had never been popular, and was increasingly viewed as a politically and morally indefensible imperial adventure. Ignored by the media under Brezhnev, the Afghan campaign received progressively franker coverage from 1983, a revealing demonstration of '*glasnost* before *glasnost*'. After 1986, regular television coverage of the war, dwelling upon the suffering of wives and mothers awaiting delivery of their slaughtered young men in 'black tulips' (plastic body-bags), made a profound impression throughout Soviet society (Remnick, 1994). Although *only* 14 000 Soviet soldiers were killed in Afghanistan, almost trivial by comparison with the twenty-seven million Soviet deaths incurred in the Second World War, a total of one million military personnel served in the campaign, with 110 000 soldiers in Afghanistan at any given time through the 1980s. The demobilised *Afghantsy* (Soviet veterans of the Afghan War) were often embittered and traumatised by their compulsory foreign service, unsettling the unappreciative Soviet society to which they returned (Keep, 1995). The patent inability of the Soviet superpower to overwhelm the *mujaheddin* in Afghanistan was as baffling and demoralising to the Russians as had been the inability of the USA to defeat the Viet Cong in Vietnam to the Americans.

The gibe that the Soviet Union, for all its pretensions to superpower glamour, was becoming an 'Upper Volta with missiles', a primitive society which vaingloriously misspent its limited wealth on glossy but unusable military hardware, was universally quoted (Remnick, 1994: 199). Yet even the vestigial pride contained within this taunt was undermined in May 1987, when a German teenager, Matthias Rust, penetrated Soviet air defences – on Border Guards' Day – to land his Cessna plane on Red Square in Moscow, a monumental embarrassment to the military establishment (Wright, 1989). From the tragedy of the Afghan War to the farce of the Rust affair, the poor showing of the Soviet armed forces was widely viewed as symptomatic of the physical collapse and spiritual demoralisation of the Soviet Union.

The most dramatic revelation of Soviet incompetence, however, was reserved for its technological performance. Forced by a shortfall of coal resources in the European Soviet Union, and a strategic pressure to reserve Siberian oil and gas for sale to eastern Europe and especially to the West for hard-currency profit, the Kremlin decided to plump for nuclear energy to supply the domestic consumer from the late 1960s. Through the 1970s, the Soviet nuclear energy programme was expanded massively in order to attempt to satisfy rocketing domestic demand for power. Unhappily, the design, construction, equipment and staffing of the Soviet RBMK-1000 pressurised-water reactors were all typical of the stagnation era and fell far below international standards of safe operation (Read, 1993).

On 26 April 1986, the Chernobyl-4 nuclear reactor, hastily constructed to supply the Kiev area of the Ukraine, exploded. The immediate repercussions of Chernobyl, soon to be revealed as the world's worst nuclear accident, are difficult to exaggerate. Radioactive fall-out, later estimated by the World Health Organisation as 200 times that of the atomic bombs dropped on Hiroshima and Nagasaki, contaminated the area, forcing the evacuation of half a million of the local population and rendering one-third of Belorussia unfit for human habitation or agricultural cultivation. As the radioactive plume circulated around Europe, necessitating the slaughter of contaminated livestock as geographically distant as reindeer in Lapland and sheep in Wales, an initial instinctive attempt at cover-up became untenable. As details of the accident were made available to and by both domestic and foreign investigating teams, the technological reputation of the Soviet Union at home and abroad was soon in tatters (Read, 1993).

The longer-term repercussions of Chernobyl could not have been more far-reaching. The clean-up by 800 000 'liquidators' and the construction of a concrete sarcophagus to seal up the radioactive reactor were achieved only at enormous financial cost. The discredited Soviet nuclear reactor programme was suspended, with planned expansion abandoned and the decommissioning of currently operative reactors placed under active consideration. The resultant power crisis across the Soviet Union forced the diversion of previously reserved oil and gas resources to internal consumption, further exacerbating the financial plight of the Soviet Empire. Within Soviet society, Chernobyl fed a hysterical atmosphere of radiophobia: communities accustomed by past censorship to fearing the worst were panicked into believing the most sensational doomsday scenarios generated

117

by local rumour factories (Read, 1993). The near meltdown of the Chernobyl nuclear core initiated a total and irreversible meltdown in mass respect for Soviet competence and, ultimately, legitimacy.

The near-apocalyptic Chernobyl accident, occurring (unluckily for Gorbachev) within three months of the announcement of the new openness, detonated an information explosion (Stokes, 1993; Keep, 1995). As if crass incompetence was not enough, revelations of gross corruption scandalised public opinion and further undermined the evaporating respectability of the Communist establishments throughout the Soviet Empire. Investigative journalism, a previously unknown Soviet phenomenon, played an especially potent role in exposing the subsidised shops, chauffeur-driven limousines, generous perks and frequent free (even foreign) holidays which sustained the generally cushioned lifestyles of the privileged, sometimes pampered Communist élites (Hosking, 1991). The notorious high-living 'socialism in one family' of the Ceausescus was revealed as not an embarrassing, uniquely Romanian aberration but just the most shameless instance of a nepotism which was endemic within what Milovan Djilas had long ago identified as a new class – the 'red bourgeoisie' of the Soviet Empire (Djilas, 1957). In higher education, for example, the best universities were in practice not open to talent regardless of social class (which officially no longer existed) but reserved for the offspring of the Soviet establishment, who succeeded the generation of their fathers in staffing the higher reaches of the state and party *apparat* (McCauley, 1981: 229). The egalitarianism and meritocracy of Soviet propaganda were shown to be in shocking contrast to the arbitrary and irresponsible power wielded by the hypocritical and self-perpetuating Soviet élites (Walker, 1993).

Most damaging of all among the exposés of *glasnost* was abundant evidence of the naked criminality of past Soviet governments. Gorbachev unwisely authorised research into hitherto taboo 'blank spots' left by official history, prompting a natural – if perhaps morbid – preoccupation with the excesses of the Stalin era (Keep, 1995). The consequent revelations administered the *coup de grâce* to the already moribund 'Friendship of Nations' doctrine originally peddled by Stalin to accompany the launch of the Soviet Empire.

The *cause célèbre* of the wartime murder of some 14 000 Poles at Katyn had always been blamed on the Nazis by the Soviet government, albeit with increasing lack of conviction. The series of grisly discoveries of mass graves in the western forests of the Ukraine and Belorussia (including some 10 000 at Vynnitsia and 30 000 at Kuropaty) during 1988–9 confirmed long-held suspicions: the cold-blooded executions of Polish élites at Katyn, now dated to March 1940, were not an uncharacteristic and exceptional 'lapse from socialist legality' but the inexcusable product of Stalinist practices common to the point of typical in the 1930s and 1940s (Keep, 1995). Research into the 'Great Terror' and man-made famine of the 1930s uncovered how the Ukrainian nation was the prime target for Stalinist oppression. Authorised historical investigations into the diplomacy of the Molotov–Ribbentrop pact of 1939 proved not only shocking to Russians raised on the sanctity of the anti-Fascist crusade but galvanised Estonians, Latvians and Lithuanians into nationalist protest against the illegal and forcible territorial incorporations of 1940. Historical *glasnost* also revealed how the brutal transportation to Siberia and central Asia of such allegedly disloyal national groups as Germans, Estonians, Latvians, Lithuanians, Belorussians, Ukrainians and various Caucasian nationalities was capped by the genocidal targeting of the Poles and Jews.

Tragically, Katyn was far from unique. As the investigative Memorial movement graphically demonstrated, most of the non-Russian nations of the Soviet Union had suffered their own individual 'Katyns' through murderous Stalinist operations which invited comparisons with the Nazi 'Final Solution' in their genocidal purpose (Remnick, 1994). The rediscovery of the recent past permitted by *glasnost* revived the nationalist campaigns of the non-Russians within the Soviet Bloc, injecting a spirit of universal protest, prompting an authoritative popular counter-culture and liquidating any vestigial sense of the legitimacy of Soviet sway.

If the Gorbachev policy of *glasnost* was a tacit recognition of the victory of the information revolution coupled with a bold attempt to control the phenomenon through official licence, there seems no doubt that this desperate stratagem of damage-limitation failed. At the very least, *glasnost* failed to channel the media revolution to the advantage of the resident Soviet establishment. Most commonly, *glasnost* backfired disastrously upon Communist authority. China, which was currently introducing its own state-sponsored *perestroika* without permitting *glasnost*, was to lambast Gorbachev both for linking *glasnost* and *perestroika* and for launching *glasnost* a year before *perestroika*. Such Kremlin misjudgement in establishing Soviet priorities inevitably resulted in a 'galloping *glasnost*', destabilising the political and social conditions in which *perestroika* should and could have worked (Keep, 1995: 415). Whatever the justice of the Chinese argument, there is little doubt that the runaway success of *glasnost* doomed *perestroika* to failure in the Soviet Union. The mounting historical and contemporary record of incompetence, corruption and criminality exposed by *glasnost* constituted an indictment which exploded both the moral legitimacy and political credibility of Communist regimes throughout the Soviet Bloc.

The Power of the Powerless

It may be true that there is nothing so irresistible as an idea whose time has come; but there is also nothing so resistible as an ideology whose time is up. The disgracing of Soviet government through *glasnost* and the impotence of the powerful in implementing their *dirigiste* vision of *perestroika* produced a political and social vacuum soon invaded by what Vaclav Havel had predicted ten years earlier as the 'power of the powerless', a civic phenomenon now reinforced by a fusion of the traditional force of nationalism and the novel force of environmentalism (Havel, 1985; Tismaneanu, 1992).

Environmentalism was immeasurably boosted but not created by Chernobyl. Local, usually unreported, protests at an unprecedented succession of Soviet eco-disasters had flared up during the early 1980s, promoting the first stirrings of an organised environmentalist movement (Hosking, 1991). Chernobyl itself was perceived as only the most dramatic in a series of 'Chernobyls'. The 'silent Chernobyl', the draining of the Aral Sea to sustain the cotton monoculture of Soviet central Asia, understandably received much shocked publicity. The appalling realisation of a 'slow Chernobyl', the broad swathe of life-threatening blight perpetrated by dinosaur smoke-stack industries running east to west from Baikal to Bitterfeld, etched itself into the broader European consciousness (Stokes, 1991; Roskin, 1994). The fresher and healthier political climate infiltrating the Soviet Bloc after 1986 ensured that the populace was now more likely to hear about threats to the environment: under *glasnost*, eco-disasters could no longer be artificially excluded from the public domain by the arbitrary exercise of state power.

The political plume and social fall-out emanating from such 'Chernobyls' were prodigious and pervasive. Concerned conservationist groups mushroomed throughout eastern Europe, many (like Ecoglasnost in Bulgaria) politically partisan. The all-too-real physical threat to the community politicised a stratum of the population which had previously been below or beyond the conventional orbit of Soviet-style politics (Hosking, 1991). By contrast to stratospherically remote Communist high politics, environmental threat introduced a new band of 'low politics' on to the political landscape, which was directly geared to the lives of involved ordinary people, lending a genuinely popular and populist dimension to protest at official stewardship of the economy, society and environment.

Nationalism within the Soviet Empire, which had never been eliminated or even reliably tamed and domesticated, only muzzled and kennelled, was always waiting for the opportunity to exploit any weakness displayed by the Communist establishment. Anger at the arbitrariness of the pollutant all-union ministries in Moscow could only be reflected in an anti-metropolitan antagonism which favoured the revival of localism, regionalism and especially nationalism. Low-profile nationalism now mobilised to pick up on the universal disquiet, articulating and exploiting mass local resentment of 'vandalistic' treatment at the hands of distant and uncaring authority. The overall effect was a blending of traditional nationalist and new environmentalist consciousness to produce a 'greening' of nationalism and a much publicised, if locally very variable, groundswell of popular protest throughout the Soviet Bloc (Crampton, 1994: 412–13).

Within the Soviet Union, the rise of green nationalism or eco-nationalism was remarkable for its patchiness. Although Chernobyl provoked widespread grass-roots anti-Russian resentment and recrimination over the worst-affected areas of Belorussia and the Ukraine, articulate protest was perhaps surprisingly slow to form: only in December 1987 was the Zelenyi Svit (Green World) organisation founded in Ukraine. By contrast, the Baltic republics of the Soviet Union, long dismayed at their demographic swamping by mass Russian immigration, were galvanised by green nationalism (Nahaylo and Swoboda, 1990). In Latvia, a demonstration in March 1988 to the mark the anniversary of the mass Soviet deportations of Latvians in 1949 displayed the broadening impact of historical *glasnost*. In Lithuania, anti-nuclear sentiment provoked by Chernobyl mounted during 1987, making a major contribution to the Sajudis movement launched in June 1988. Popular demonstrations against the Ignalina nuclear plant in September 1988 pressured the Latvian parliament into declaring that Latvian alone was the official language of Latvia from November 1988. In Estonia, television debates inspired by *glasnost* throughout 1987 led to the foundation of the Popular Front for Perestroika in April 1988. In November 1988, the Estonian parliament dared to declare the sovereignty of Estonia, a provocative nationalist act of defiance which was to be replicated in all parts of the Soviet Union by mid-1990. The Baltic republics were identified over 1987–8 as the champions of an environmentalist-cum-nationalist campaign which threatened to pervade and eventually destabilise the entire inner empire of the Soviet Union (Hosking, 1991; Keep, 1995).

People-Power

If the most westerly (and Western) parts of the Soviet Union were being persuaded of the 'power of the powerless', the outer empire of eastern Europe, long sensitised by the events of 1956, 1968 and 1980, was wielding what was increasingly called 'people-power'. The Iron Curtain, the most symbolic artefact of an obsolescent Yalta Europe, was being afflicted by extensive and irreversible metal fatigue. Mass tourism alone, promoted to earn desperately needed hard currency, ensured that by the mid-1980s the Iron Curtain represented only a translucent filter to communication between East and West. With the number of privately owned radios and especially television receivers increasing out of all regulation, modern broadcasting mocked the barbed wire of land frontiers. As Intervision, the broadcasting cartel of the Soviet Bloc, lost its reception monopoly across eastern Europe, the social role of television switched from general anaesthetic through prescriptive sedative to unrestricted stimulant. As Estonians settled down to watch Finnish TV, East Germans and Czechs discovered West German TV, Slovenes and Croats tuned in to Italian TV, and Hungarians and Slovaks eavesdropped on Austrian TV, the bulk of the peoples of eastern Europe could no longer be kept ignorant of freer and richer societies to the west (Crampton, 1994).

Understandably, many east Europeans were misled by what they learned – or thought they were learning – through the *televorot* (TV revolution) about the quality of everyday life in western Europe and beyond. What has been dubbed the 'Dallas complex', by which people in the East believed that everybody in the West lived like a Texas oil baron, had the effect of creating a consumerism of envy, raising expectations unrealistically high. Even so, genuine comparisons between Eastern and Western standards of living were drawn, sometimes with traumatic effects. A celebrated example of the prosperity gap was the Kit-E-Kat scandal of February 1988, when a well-meaning Anglo-Soviet TV link-up with an unedited commercial break inadvertently revealed to the outraged population of Moscow that British felines had daily access to more and better meat than Soviet humans.

As usual, the latest crisis at the Soviet imperial centre had its deepest resonance in colonial eastern Europe. Gorbachev's attempt at first reform from above and then revolution from above was challenged first by reform from below and eventually by people-power revolution from below.

The two ice-breakers of Cold War eastern Europe – Hungary and Poland – seized the initiative for fundamental change through 1988 and 1989. But although both calculatedly chose courses occupying the middle ground between reform and revolution, which have been dubbed 'refolution' or 'revorm', each opted for individual campaigns with differing reforming or revolutionary emphases (Garton Ash, 1989: 309; Tismaneanu, 1992).

With the ousting of the veteran Kadar from power in May 1988, Hungary followed an evolutionary reforming path under the new, economically pragmatic leadership of Karolyi Grosz, dubbed the 'Hungarian Gorbachev'. Even so, the reforming Hungarian establishment was soon drawn into actions which effected a 'negotiated revolution' (Stokes, 1993: 132). In February 1989, the Hungarian Communist party, now dominated by radical reformers headed by Imre Pozsgay, indulged in a spectacular exercise in historical *glasnost* by acknowledging that '1956' had been not a counter-revolution but a mass popular uprising. Since this public admission was by implication an attack on its own legitimacy, the Hungarian establishment took the bold step of renouncing its power monopoly and admitting a multi-party system in Hungary for the future (Garton Ash, 1990; Stokes, 1991).

Hungary provocatively went even further in May 1989 by dismantling its section of the Iron Curtain (Glenny, 1990). The official explanation that the fortified Hungarian border was 'too expensive to maintain' was patently unconvincing but contained a broader truth: the financial and personnel costs of ring-fencing the Soviet Empire were becoming politically prohibitive. For so long the Soviet colony which had most adroitly straddled the uncomfortable economic and social divide between communism and capitalism, Hungary led the way in liquidating the physical barrier separating eastern from western Europe.

Poland followed a more confrontational path even before 1989. Faced with summer-long general strikes, the defensive Communist establishment of Jaruzelski was forced to negotiate with the Solidarity of Walesa from as early as August 1988. After months of protracted discussions, a re-legalised Solidarity and the Polish government reached a compromise 'Round Table Accord' in April 1989: in the upcoming general election, 35 per cent of the seats in the *Sejm* and all the seats in the new Senate (the lower and upper chambers of the Polish Parliament) could be contested by non-official candidates. Although the government could not be numerically outvoted under such an arrangement, it could – and did – suffer a moral and political defeat. At the general election in June 1989, Solidarity enjoyed a landslide victory by capturing all but one of the seats that it was permitted to contest (Garton Ash, 1990). The popular mandate for Solidarity was undeniable, threatening an ungovernable Poland. In August 1989, after further anguished negotiations, Jaruzelski conceded an administration headed by Tadeusz Mazowiecki, a leader of Solidarity (Swain, 1993; Stokes, 1991). The first non-Communist-led government since the late 1940s took power in Soviet eastern Europe.

The Hungarian and Polish acts of defiance of the Soviet Empire, attacking the very essence of Yalta Europe, were followed by the supreme demonstration of people-power in the 'state without a nation' – East Germany (Brown, 1991: 125). During September 1989, East Germans recognised that the Hungarian breaching of the Iron Curtain opened up a backstairs route to unofficial emigration, prompting an exodus of predominantly young and professional East Germans via Czechoslovakia and Hungary to Austria and West Germany. Indignant complaints by the East German government at their neighbours' lack of 'fraternal socialist solidarity' were followed by demands that this brain-drain to the West be plugged. With its protests pointedly ignored by Hungary, East Germany had little option but to adopt the desperate and hazardous recourse of closing its own frontiers (Dunbabin, 1994).

The tacit vote of no-confidence in East Germany implicit in the traffic-jam to emigrate was topped in October 1989 by overt popular protest at official celebrations of the fortieth anniversary of the German Democratic Republic. Starting in Leipzig and spreading to other major cities of East Germany, street demonstrations on an unprecedented scale thundered mass condemnation of the resident Communist regime (Garton Ash, 1990; Tismaneanu, 1992). East Germany was overhauling the Hungarian and Polish front-runners of radical change: two distinct mass demonstrations of East Germans voting with their feet precipitated the definitive test-case for the maintenance of the Soviet Empire in eastern Europe.

Beating Retreat

Although October 1989 was to prove the decisive turning-point for eastern Europe, the eye-catching 'triumph of the powerless' should not entirely distract historical attention away from the willingness of Gorbachev to countenance the decolonisation of the outer empire (Tismaneanu, 1992: 175). Initially, Gorbachev clearly hoped to persuade the eastern European regimes to follow the Soviet example in converting to *glasnost* and *perestroika*. Some leaderships, like the Jaruzelski and Kadar establishments in Poland and Hungary, expressed guarded acquiescence. Others, notably Honecker in East Germany and especially Husak in Czechoslovakia in March 1986, made their reluctance to fall into line unequivocal (Swain, 1993). During an uncomfortable state visit to Romania in May 1987, Gorbachev was informed that his host had been implementing *perestroika* since the 1960s and therefore Ceausescu and not the Soviet leader deserved the accolade of 'creator of *perestroika*' (Wright, 1989). The recalcitrance of most of the eastern European older-generation 'colonial governors' provides an insight into the decline in Kremlin authority over the outer empire during the forty years since the heady days of High Stalinism.

By 1988, Gorbachev was effectively confronted by two imperial options. First, to impose *perestroika* on the neo-Stalinist eastern European establishments, a bizarre perversion of the Brezhnev Doctrine of legitimate Soviet intervention. Such a high-risk course would necessarily involve a prohibitively expensive investment of military force at a time when the pruning of the military budget had the highest overall priority. Such a no-win option, inevitably involving the scuppering of the charm offensive which was proving so successful in the West, could only be rejected. The second option was to insinuate *perestroika* covertly, employing Soviet influence to undermine hardline establishments and favour more progressive elements within the eastern European Communist cadres (Tismaneanu, 1992). This preferred *perestroika*-by-conspiracy option, arguably most evident in Gorbachev's relations with Bulgaria and Czechoslovakia, was dramatically overtaken by the accelerating momentum of people-power through eastern Europe in the course of 1989 (Fernandez-Armesto, 1995; Roskin, 1994).

By autumn 1989, the stark choice for Gorbachev, bearing the supreme responsibility for the fate of the Soviet Empire, was reduced to either military-based intervention and repression, as demonstrated on Tiananmen Square in Peking just a few months previously, or acceptance of imperial decolonisation. Gorbachev was lobbied uninhibitedly by champions of both mutually exclusive options: demanding an Eastern-style crackdown was the hard-pressed East German premier Erich Honecker; proposing a Western-style decolonisation of eastern Europe was the pragmatic Soviet foreign minister Eduard Shevarnadze (Dunbabin, 1994; Roskin, 1994).

The military intervention option indulged in 1956 and 1968 had not been employed in 1980–1, an indication of its declining popularity within Kremlin decision-making circles even under Brezhnev. Moreover, the protracted Afghan war had both damaged the morale of the Soviet armed forces and undermined Kremlin confidence in military so-called solutions to essentially political crises. Visiting Peking at the time of the Tiananmen Square massacre in June 1989, Gorbachev came away convinced of the necessity of making a clear distinction between 'Chinese' and 'Russian' responses to manifestations of people-power. Militarily, politically and financially, the prospect of attempting a crackdown simultaneously in Hungary, Poland and East Germany was too daunting to be a viable option.

The decolonisation option had in practice been adopted by Gorbachev well in advance of the supreme crisis of October 1989. A full year before, in September 1988, Gorbachev closed down the CPSU's liaison committee with socialist countries, a coded signalling to Communist establishments of Soviet abandonment of the Brezhnev Doctrine (Swain, 1993). In December 1988, Gorbachev promised the General Assemby of the United Nations unilateral cuts of 500 000 Soviet troops, one-half of them in eastern Europe (Simons, 1993; Walker, 1993). By July 1989, Gorbachev was urging a Warsaw Pact meeting in Budapest to adopt 'independent solutions to national problems' and announcing to the Council of Europe at Strasbourg recognition of eastern Europeans' right 'to seek their own destinies in a common European home' (Stokes, 1991; Simons, 1993). Such indicators of Soviet complaisance naturally encouraged Hungary and Poland to raise the horizons of their ambition. Gorbachev may not have created the developing crisis; but his increasingly conciliatory attitude towards eastern European people-power (not to mention his earlier responsibility for launching *glasnost*) made a crucial contribution to the supreme imperial crisis of October 1989.

Gorbachev's attitude towards the outer empire of the Soviet Bloc bears comparison with the decolonisation of more traditional Western empires. Though few ex-colonies care to advertise the fact, empires commonly retreat as much for reasons of economic retrenchment as forcible expulsion by irresistible emancipation movements. National emancipators predictably claim the push-out of alien empire but imperialists are more often persuaded by the financial advantages offered by an expedient pull-out. Colonies have always had an irritating tendency to start as assets but end up as liabilities which the imperial power is increasingly tempted to offload. After 1985, Gorbachev was progressively constrained to confront the supreme issue of imperial cost-benefit fudged for decades by his predecessors: to cut imperial losses by shedding an eastern Europe which had become more trouble than it was worth to the Soviet Union.

Gorbachev went public over his decision to accept without protest or rancour the 'rolling decolonisation' of the outer empire over the third week of October 1989. In East Germany, Honecker's instinct to counter the growing demonstrations in Leipzig, Dresden and East Berlin by military suppression was vetoed by the Kremlin. On 23 October, two statements of supreme political significance were delivered: in Budapest, Hungary declared itself a sovereign independent republic, the first east European state formally to renounce all vestiges of Soviet colonial status; in Moscow, Shevarnadze announced to the Soviet Congress of People's Deputies 'the impermissibility of any interference' by the Soviet Union in the affairs of eastern Europe. Instantly and memorably trivialised by Gorbachev's foreign affairs spokesman Gennadii Gerasimov as the 'Sinatra Doctrine', explicit Soviet permission for eastern Europeans 'to do things their way' sanctioned the revolutions already accomplished in Hungary and Poland, encouraged the ongoing revolution in East Germany and primed revolutions in Bulgaria, Czechoslovakia and Romania (Tismaneanu, 1992).

If there were any lingering doubts about Gorbachev's politic complaisance towards the now-irresistible wave of revolutions transforming the outer empire, they were laid to rest on a state visit to Finland on 25 October. Anxious to avoid torpedoing the imminent Malta Summit with Reagan by any repressive actions against rampant people-power, Gorbachev delivered an unequivocal Kremlin repudiation of the Brezhnev Doctrine in operation since the Warsaw Pact invasion of Czechoslovakia in 1968. To repeat a contemporary Russian joke, the Moscow emergency phone number for fraternal assistance (56-68-81) was taken out of service (Simons, 1993: 199).

The symbolism of place in Gorbachev's momentous announcement in Helsinki could hardly have been more poignant or ironic. For decades, Western 'Cold Warriors' had pointed to Finland as the ignominious best that any nation neighbouring the Soviet Union could expect by way of treatment. The pejorative and contemptuous term 'Finlandisation' was coined to describe a nation's craven kowtowing to every Soviet whim to preserve the empty trappings of nominal sovereignty. Over the years since 1945, Finland had made concessions which critics argued made a mockery of sovereignty and effectively rendered the state an informal colony of the Soviet outer empire. In 1975, 'Helsinki' meant international endorsement of the Soviet Empire and tacit recognition of the Brezhnev Doctrine of imperial intervention. At the same time, Helsinki '75 also included the formal Soviet promise of observance of civil rights, which provided the legitimacy for a dissident movement which was to articulate the people-power of the late 1980s. In 1989 came first the prospect of the whole of the Soviet outer empire becoming 'Finlandised', then the realisation that 'Finlandisation' itself was being consigned to the imperial past. In stark contrast to Helsinki '75, a green light for the comprehensive decolonisation of eastern Europe was flashed by Helsinki '89.

Landslide and Timeslip

In late 1989, the tectonic plate of eastern Europe experienced a seismic shift unprecedented since the Second World War: an earthquake which registered at the very top of the geopolitical Richter scale detached almost half a continent from the imperial authority of the Kremlin.

By late October 1989, Hungary was officially and Poland was effectively independent, with the Sinatra Doctrine retrospectively legalising a diplomatic *fait accompli*. In early November, the crisis in East Germany reached its climax. Abandoned by Gorbachev, the hardline Honecker was ditched in favour of the more conciliatory Egon Krenz. At midnight on 8/9 November, in an episode which combined spontaneous people-power with impromptu official resignation, the Berlin Wall was breached: elated crowds in East Berlin surged past bemused frontier guards to make a mass visit to West Berlin that had been impossible for almost thirty years (Stokes, 1991).

The symbolic impact of the 'fall' of the Berlin Wall upon eastern Europe is almost impossible to overplay. The self-confidence of people-power was immeasurably enhanced, delivering the *coup de grâce* to the already tattered self-respect of the remaining Communist regimes. The nerve of governments confronted by mass opposition, which dared authority to exercise the Tiananmen option of naked repression before a global audience, cracked and disintegrated. Thrown on to the political defensive, shamed and demoralised establishments lost the will to govern, succumbed to defeatist resignation and surrendered power (Tismaneanu, 1992). As a demonstration effect of people-power captured the public imagination, the accelerating momentum of change made each revolution faster than its predecessor, effecting a 'domino collapse' of Soviet-dependent regimes across eastern Europe (Roskin, 1994: 136).

Bulgaria, the most consistently obsequious of all colonies within the Soviet Empire, was next to go. With the closest historical links to Russia, Bulgaria's unconditional loyalty to Moscow was legendary. It was reliably rumoured that Todor Zhivkov, in power since 1954 and therefore the longest-serving premier in eastern Europe, applied for Bulgaria to become the sixteenth union republic of the Soviet Union at the time of the drafting of the Soviet Constitution of 1977. From the mid-1980s, Zhivkov promoted his own national *perestroika*, a socialist 'regenerative process' whose principal feature was harassment of the substantial Turkish minority in Bulgaria (Stokes, 1993). Exploiting the hostile international press which greeted the part-exodus, part-expulsion of some 300 000 Turks from Bulgaria over the summer of 1989, a conspiracy headed by Petar Mladenov prudently secured Kremlin approval before ousting Zhivkov from power in mid-November (Glenny, 1990; Roskin, 1994). Though more a palace *coup* than a triumph for people-power, the self-proclaimed 'gentle revolution' promised a definitive break with the Communist past (Tismaneanu, 1992).

In Czechoslovakia, the post-Prague Spring culling of the more vigorous and talented of Communist personnel had promoted less a 'normalisation' than a 'stupidisation' of government (Simons, 1993: 218). The two-year hardline regime of Milos Jakes, who had administered the post-1968 purges, softened during 1989 as its Hungarian and Polish neighbours accelerated along the road to independence from Moscow. A popular demonstration on the anniversary of the Warsaw Pact invasion in August 1989 was nervously ignored by the authorities. Following the gratuitously vicious police suppression of a student rally in Prague on 17 November, the Czech Civic Forum and the Slovak Public Against Violence were formed, dissident-led organisations providing a focus for mass opposition (Garton Ash, 1990). There is evidence that an attempted palace revolution on the *perestroika*-by-stealth model was bungled, so fundamentally disconcerting the Communist establishment that no resistance against the popular groundswell could be mounted (Dunbabin, 1994). By late December, the demoralised government had resigned in a 'velvet revolution' which carried Vaclav Havel, the leader of Charter 77, and Alexander Dubcek, the Communist martyr of 1968, jointly into power in Czechoslovakia (Glenny, 1990; Tismaneanu, 1992).

Last in line for revolution, if only because of the intimidating reputation of its *Securitate*, was Romania. Ceausescu became obsessed with repaying Romania's debts to the West, but this admirable fiscal objective was achieved only by the politically hazardous stratagem of penalising the general populace by a state-enforced collapse in living standards (Schopflin, 1993). Clumsy *Securitate* moves to evict Pastor Laszlo Tokes, the spokesman for the indigenous Hungarian minority in the provincial city of Timosoara, outraged the local populace into mass protest, precipitating first an army massacre and then a crisis of provincial government (Stokes, 1993). Establishment second-rankers like Ion Iliescu, eager to be rid of the overbearing (and since 1982 officially divine) Nicolae and Elena Ceausescu, exploited a rare opportunity for self-advancement. The developing December drama was flashed to TV viewers around the world: a Bucharest crowd assembled to applaud the *Conducator* instead heckled the astounded 'hero of the Carpathians', who resorted to ignominious escape from the roof of his palace by helicopter. The flight of the Ceausescus ended with their capture, mock trial and summary execution by firing squad (Swain, 1993). Part demonstration of pent-up people-power, part opportunist palace *coup*, the 'Christmas Revolution' in Romania completed a clean sweep of the eastern European Communist *ancien régime* within the Soviet Empire.

Epic in scale and breathtaking in pace, the serial revolution surging through autumn 1989 was the culmination of a 'long rebellion against Yalta' which brought to an abrupt end the forty-year era of Soviet 'satellisation' of eastern Europe (Tismaneanu, 1992: 281). Under mounting pressure from eastern European people-power, Gorbachev's decision to switch from Brezhnev Doctrine to Sinatra Doctrine part legitimised, part promoted the comprehensive decolonisation of the Soviet outer empire and the rolling dissolution of the Yalta Europe bequeathed by the Second World War.

7

MOSCOW 1991:
DISINTEGRATION
OF THE INNER EMPIRE

The sudden decolonisation of the outer empire of the Soviet Bloc was greeted with transparent astonishment but then uncontainable glee by the West. Extravagant claims were made by commentators attempting to comprehend the long-term significance of what was agreed to be an historical watershed. Many historians identified an *annus mirabilis* which rendered 1989 comparable to 1789 as a turning-point in world history, with one going so far as to announce the 'End of History': the imminent global collapse of communism represented the triumph of the West and a definitive and permanent victory for Western democratic values and the capitalist economic order (Fukuyama, 1989).

To many 'Cold Warriors', democracy in eastern Europe had prevailed within the context of Western confrontation but without the necessity of Western intervention: the walls of the morally bankrupt, politically discredited Communist Jericho had come tumbling down under the trumpet blasts of indigenous people-power. To others, the Cold War was finally drawing to a close. The meteorological fact that the Russian winter of 1989 was the mildest for over a century (since 1882 indeed) was a coincidental, trite but telling symbol of permanent thaw in the Stalinist Cold War empire and therefore of global warming in international relations. The West took for granted the inexorable easterly advance of democracy and capitalism, the unavoidable eastward retreat of communism and the inevitable liquidation of the remaining inner empire of the Soviet Union.

To Gorbachev, however, the 'Year of Miracles' did not necessarily mean either the collapse of communism or the inescapable doom of the Soviet Union (Walker, 1994). For Gorbachev, whose definitions of 'eastern Europe' and the 'Soviet Union' were obdurately dated from 1945, the border of the Soviet Union was sacrosanct and non-negotiable. Before, during and after the momentous events of 1989, the Soviet leader repeatedly underscored the absolute distinction which he drew between what was permissible outside and within Soviet jurisdiction (Remnick, 1994). Gorbachev may have had the effective decolonisation of eastern Europe foisted upon him but this expedient geopolitical retrenchment made him all the more determined to retain Soviet authority in the territory remaining. The tidal wave of national 'rollback' may have washed irresistibly over the outer empire but it would not be allowed to breach the sea wall of the Soviet Union.

Soviet Disunion

While the year 1989 transformed eastern Europe, people-power was still in the process of establishing itself within the Soviet Union. As the only sovereign states of the interwar period to have suffered full incorporation into the postwar Soviet Union, Estonia, Latvia and Lithuania were always going to be the champions of separatism. Arguing the indefensible illegality of the 1939 Molotov–Ribbentrop Pact which 'authorised' Soviet absorption of the independent Baltic States in 1940, nationalist campaigners demanded the righting of the *diktat* inflicted on Estonia, Latvia and Lithuania by Hitler and Stalin, and their return to post-Soviet eastern Europe. To this end, the Baltic republics represented themselves 'with dour cunning' as a special case for 're-sovereignisation' which need not be regarded as a test-case for the broader decolonisation of the Soviet Union

(Hosking, 1991: 191). Gorbachev's reaction was that, notwithstanding the acknowledged unique predicament of Estonia, Latvia and Lithuania, no exceptions could be made for any of the union republics, for the integrity of the Soviet Union took automatic precedence over all sectional and national interests. No matter how unjustly, the Baltic application was in practice already viewed as a test-case for all other union republics, who would instantly clamour for similar treatment should the collective Baltic petition be successful.

The environmentalist-cum-nationalist Baltic (re)awakening of 1987–8 accordingly gathered momentum during 1989. The political drama unfolding in neighbouring Poland, culminating in the stunning victory of Solidarity in the June general election, inspired the Lithuanian Sajudis organisation in particular to step up its public pressure. The most spectacular propaganda *coup* for Baltic people-power came in August 1989. Anniversaries have always preoccupied the nations of eastern Europe, for whom the vicissitudes of recent history retain a vibrant contemporary resonance. The fiftieth anniversary of the hated Molotov–Ribbentrop Pact was commemorated by a north–south 'Freedom Chain' connecting the Baltic capitals of Tallinn, Riga and Vilnius, a mass demonstration of popular commitment by Estonians, Latvians and Lithuanians turning their collective eyes to the West and their eloquent backs to the Soviet East (Remnick, 1994).

Despite efforts to buy off Baltic dissidence, notably by the Supreme Soviet in July 1989 granting 'economic autonomy' to Estonia, Latvia and Lithuania from 1990, it was already too late. Concessions which might have stood a chance of containing Baltic nationalism up to 1987 and possibly 1988 now only whetted the Baltic appetite for more. By August 1989 a worried *Pravda* was denouncing the nationalist hysteria in the Baltic and ordering the local Communist establishments to squash 'extremism and separatism'. But as revolution swept Hungary, Poland, East Germany, Bulgaria, Czechoslovakia and Romania during autumn 1989, the Baltic nations made no secret of their determination to participate in the re-creation of an independent eastern Europe (Nahaylo and Swoboda, 1990).

Although Estonia, Latvia and Lithuania were the first to campaign for independence, they became only the leaders in a lengthening queue during 1989. In the Moldavian Union Republic, an autonomist movement raised its head from January 1989, arguing (like the Baltic nations) that Moldavian Romanians were a special case requiring prompt restorative action. As the most northerly province of interwar 'Greater Romania', Moldavia had been unceremoniously absorbed into the Soviet Union, initially by the same squalid Nazi–Soviet deal which had terminated independent Estonia, Latvia and Lithuania. Only the grotesquely unappealing prospect of reincorporation into the *Securitate*-ridden Romania of Ceausescu kept the Moldavian Popular Front, founded in May 1989, restricting its campaign to greater autonomy within the Soviet Union (Nahaylo and Swoboda, 1990). Once the Ceausescu regime crumbled in the 'Christmas Revolution' of 1989, Moldavians were tempted to switch their allegiance to territorial reunion with the new Romania and cling to Baltic coat-tails in seeking independence from the Soviet Union (Hosking, 1991; Keep, 1995).

With the inspirational, if ephemeral, experiences of independence enjoyed by Armenia, Azerbaidzhan and Georgia over the Russian Civil War period, an upswing in Trans-Caucasian nationalism was always predictable. A political and social chain reaction in 1988–9 revealed just how precarious was the *pax sovietica* in the Trans-Caucasus. Significantly for the policing of local inter-ethnic relations, the Trans-Caucasian republics included the demographically smallest Russian presence of all the non-Russian union republics. The Nagorno-Karabakh crisis which blew up in February 1988 (and has smouldered without resolution ever since) proved the catalyst for first an Armenian and then an Azeri nationalist upsurge (Nahaylo and Swoboda, 1990). By autumn 1988, the political agitation engendered by the coincidence of the weakness of the republican establishments, currently suffering a Gorbachev-inspired anti-corruption investigation, and chronic inter-ethnic violence, had spilled over into Georgia (Keep, 1995). Although mass demonstrations articulating a mounting preference for independence began in February

1989, it was the unprovoked massacre of female protesters in the Georgian capital of Tbilisi in April which transformed the attitude of the Georgian nation (Hosking, 1991). If the massacre was intended to warn off Georgia from seeking independence, then that warning backfired: Georgian nationalism was inflamed, instituting a simmering resentment of not just Soviet but specifically Russian authority.

Related problems dogged the central Asian republics of the Soviet Union. The Brezhnev strategy of *korenizatsia* (indigenisation) had accustomed many local nationalities to preferential treatment over education and employment, a system of positive discrimination whose suspension under Gorbachev was greatly resented by spoiled local republican cadres. Within months of his takeover, Gorbachev was conducting a rolling purge of corruption in the mafia-like establishments of the union republics (McAuley, 1992). Subsequent revelations about the Brezhnev-licensed 'fiefdoms' of Dinmukhamed Kunayev in Kazakhstan and Sharaf Rashidov in Uzbekistan left no doubt about the prevalence of local corruption, at its most flamboyant in the traditional societies of Soviet central Asia (Hosking, 1991; Keep, 1995). Although separatist nationalism was still in its infancy, Gorbachev's disciplining of union republican leaderships in central Asia had the effect of undermining their self-confidence, letting slip the initiative to unofficial political and social elements.

Much more ominously for Soviet authority, the Ukraine at last showed signs of embracing people-power. While resistance to Soviet assimilation had undoubtedly been more obstinate than in Belorussia (as the Shelest period from 1963 to 1972 demonstrated), the Ukraine experienced difficulties in making the crucial breakthrough from passive, defensive, ethnic consciousness to offensive, militant nationalism. It is arguable that although – or perhaps because – Ukrainians were the principal victims of both Stalin and Chernobyl, the Ukraine was the last major region of the Soviet Union to experience either *glasnost* or *perestroika*, such was the grip of the last Brezhnevite party boss Vladimir Shcherbitsky and the reluctance of Gorbachev to oust

139

such a reliable viceroy. Despite the wash of Solidarity spillover from neighbouring Poland, it was not until September 1989 that two events transformed the local political scene: the founding congress of the Ukrainian popular front organisation, Rukh; and the final sacking of Gorbachev's now-embarrassing 'pet dinosaur' Shcherbitsky from the Politburo and the Ukrainian party leadership (Nahaylo and Swoboda, 1990). The second-largest union republic and the key non-Russian republic for the future of the Soviet Union, the Ukraine was crossing a Rubicon in its long-stalled political career.

The dangers of *glasnost* without *perestroika* were now only too apparent. Half-hearted attempts by Gorbachev at creating more consensus and stability only succeeded in further weakening the authority of Soviet government. A newly constituted, allegedly democratic Soviet Congress of People's Deputies turned into a spectacular public relations disaster (Walker, 1993). For the first general election to the Congress in March 1989, multi-candidate but not multi-party electoral lists were permitted, while the CPSU reserved one-third of all seats for safe establishment organs like the *Komsomol* (Communist Youth Organisation) and the Soviet Writers' Union. The electorate seized this unprecedented opportunity to express its dissatisfaction with a CPSU establishment which demonstrated crass ineptitude in fighting a general election campaign (McAuley, 1992). After the opening of the Congress in May, the televised parliamentary sessions became compulsive viewing. Absenteeism rocketed and industrial production nosedived as the Russian work force downed tools to monitor the performance of its political masters. Most workers were conspicuously unimpressed: although extended live coverage was hastily replaced by edited highlights, exposure to the unpitying eye of the TV camera inflicted serious damage on the credibility of both Congress and government (Hosking, 1991). By autumn 1989, the Congress debates had become a byword for parliamentary bluster and government impotence, enlivened only by clashes between Gorbachev and Andrei Sakharov. With the death of the 'conscience of the Russian nation' in December 1989, Gorbachev was fortunate to lose his

140

most prestigious critic but could salvage no popular respect for the beleaguered Soviet establishment (Remnick, 1994).

While separatist national sentiment mounted among the non-Russians, the Russians within and outside Russia, by far the largest of the union republics, were simultaneously undergoing a profound crisis of faith about 'their' inner empire of the Soviet Union. The sudden and bewildering loss of the outer empire during autumn 1989 confronted the Russians with two pressing imperial issues. First, was it *possible* to retain the Soviet Union? If it had proved impossible to seal off eastern Europe from western Europe before 1989, what were the realistic chances of creating a hermetic seal between the Soviet Union and newly independent eastern Europe? Virtually all the leading nations of the Soviet Union knew of the epoch-making developments to the West, wanted to share the '1989 experience' and hoped to earn the same decolonising treatment as eastern Europe (Hosking, 1991; Brown, 1991). Could the rolling decolonisation which had already transformed the outer empire of eastern Europe be prevented from sweeping irresistibly through the inner empire of the Soviet Union?

The second question followed logically: was it *desirable* to retain the Soviet Union? A variety of factors publicised by *glasnost* was cumulatively sapping the imperial will of the Russians. The most obvious was the part-expulsion, part-withdrawal from eastern Europe, which retrospectively designated the entire 1945–89 period as an episode of imperial failure. The move towards the economic decolonisation of eastern Europe over the 1970s, now perceived as a prelude to the political decolonisation of the 1980s, was paralleled by demographic decolonisation within the Soviet Union. Before the mid-1970s, Russians served in various imperial capacities across the skirting colonies of the inner empire, effecting an annual net Russian out-migration from Russia to the colonial periphery. But from the late 1970s, Russians preferred to return from service in colonial central Asia, collectively embodying an annual net Russian in-migration from the Asiatic periphery back to Russia and the European colonies (Keep, 1995). Although an astronomical twenty-five million Russians were still resident outside Russia in 1989, the mid-1970s represented a demographic watershed for the Soviet Union: thereafter, an accelerating withdrawal of Russians from the imperial periphery back to the Russian heartland was reversing the demographic colonisation characteristic of the Soviet (and indeed tsarist) past. For some fifteen years, Russians had been voting with their feet against the responsibilities of Soviet Empire.

The slump (or at least slide) in Russian commitment to the inner empire was particularly noticeable with regard to Soviet central Asia. The 1989 Soviet Census confirmed long-held Russian fears of a demographic time-bomb: with the birth-rate of many non-Russians and especially central Asians greatly exceeding that of the Russians for decades, Russians now made up barely one-half of the Soviet population, a proportion which would dip sharply in the immediate future. Soviet statisticians estimated that as soon as 1995, conscripts to the army would be only one-third Russian but also one-third Muslim (Nahaylo and Swoboda, 1990). With *Homo islamicus* threatening to overhaul *Homo sovieticus*, many Russians were deeply unhappy about the so- called 'yellowing' of a Soviet Union which was becoming proportionately less European and more Asiatic in its composition. The loss of the outer empire in 1989 severely damaged the European orientation and drastically reduced the European composition of the Soviet Bloc, compelling Russians to reconsider their attitude to the 'Russian Raj' of central Asia within the inner empire of the Soviet Union.

By the end of 1989, Russian imperial commitment was eroding fast. Russians resident in the non-Russian republics of the Soviet Union were becoming uneasy at the possibility of being left stranded in isolated enclaves within newly independent states by the territorial shrinkage of the inner empire (Keep, 1995). Should 'outposted' Russians join local nationalist popular fronts and hope to earn indulgent treatment from their new masters or form Russian interfronts to hold the Soviet Union together in a spirit of internationalisation? Within Russia itself, talk grew of withdrawing not just from the outer empire of eastern Europe but from at least part of the inner empire of the Soviet Union

(Hosking, 1991). Some ultra-nationalists went so far as to propose the shedding of all non-Russian territories and the contraction of the state back to the borders of Russia alone. For those who found this projected reversal of the last three centuries of Russian expansionism intolerable, many advocated the middle course of a shedding of all non-Slav properties, a territorial compaction into a Slavic Union composed of Russia, the Ukraine and Belorussia. 1989 closed with not only the decolonisation of the outer empire of eastern Europe but an upsurge of nationalism and a collapse of imperial will which raised the prospect of the decolonisation of the inner empire of the Soviet Union.

Imperial Implosion

The year 1990 dawned with a fresh crisis for Gorbachev, as usual provoked by the Baltic republics. Despite a conciliatory declaration by the Supreme Soviet of the USSR recognising the illegality of the Nazi–Soviet Pact of 1939, the Lithuanian Supreme Soviet decided both to license non-Communist parties and authorise a multi-party system within its jurisdiction. Fearing political annihilation, the Lithuanian Communist party issued a unilateral declaration of independence from the CPSU in December 1989, a secessionist act which was to spark a chain-reaction effecting a fatal fragmentation of the previously mono-lithic Communist establishment of the Soviet Union (Hosking, 1991; Nahaylo and Swoboda, 1990: 344).

After a fruitless visit to Lithuania in January 1990, when he signally failed to dissuade local Communists from their tactical separatism, Gorbachev decided not only to abandon resistance to the 'Lithuanian trend' but, in a dramatic strategic volte-face, to place himself at its head (Remnick, 1994). The Soviet leader was probably also strongly influenced by a similar decision made by the Yugoslav League of Communists meeting at their XIV Congress in January to relinquish their 'leading role' in Yugoslavia. In February 1990, a new course under the slogan of *demokratizatsia* was launched. In a spirit of ostensibly self-sacrificing but actually self-serving 'democratisation', the CPSU renounced its own time-hallowed monopoly of power and permitted legal non-Communist parties and activities throughout the Soviet Union. Clause Six of the Soviet Constitution guaranteeing the exclusive monopoly position of the CPSU was rescinded, a bold decision by Gorbachev to swim with the prevailing current of radical change and 'go for broke' on reform (Roskin, 1994).

The momentous self-denying declaration by the CPSU had minimal impact upon the rising groundswell of nationalism over the Soviet Union. Despite Gorbachev's assurances, faith in the Soviet government was now at a low ebb. An army massacre of over 150 Azeri nationalist demonstrators in Baku in January 1990 was perceived by many as a desperate mini-Tiananmen, suggesting that Gorbachev was either hypocritical in his promises or losing control of events (Hosking, 1991). In either case, Gorbachev could not be trusted. Elections to republican parliaments in March 1990 produced majorities for national independence in Lithuania, Latvia, Estonia and Moldavia. Accepting this popular mandate with impolitic haste, Lithuania immediately declared its independence from the Soviet Union, setting an example for all other union republics to emulate (Keep, 1995).

There could now be no mistaking the danger of a mass decolonisation of the Soviet Union. While not prepared to risk direct election from the Soviet electorate, Gorbachev had himself elected new-style executive President of the Soviet Union by the Supreme Soviet in March in order to counter the threat (McAuley, 1992; Walker, 1993). The unsatisfactoriness of the current constitution was conceded and a Soviet committee was appointed under Gorbachev's chairmanship to negotiate a new Union treaty (Hosking, 1991). Formally announced at the XXVIII Congress of the CPSU in July 1990, the renegotiation of the terms of relationship between the fifteen union republics was premised upon the admission that fundamental change was needed for the Soviet Union to survive.

The five-year anniversary in March 1990 of the accession of Mikhail Gorbachev to supreme power marks an appropriate juncture to pause in the historical narrative to consider his personal responsibility for the constitutional crisis in the Soviet inner empire. The point on which almost all commentators have agreed is that his performance was generally marked by sins of omission rather than sins of commission (Brown, 1991). The first major occasion for Gorbachev to make a pre-emptive policy statement on the imperial issue came at the XXVII CPSU Congress in February 1986. Not only was the opportunity missed but the accompanying revised edition of the Third CPSU Programme included the astonishing statement that 'the national question, a legacy of the past, has been successfully solved in the Soviet Union', a claim so preposterous as to be wantonly provocative (Nahaylo and Swoboda, 1990).

Gorbachev maintained his self-satisfied line through 1987, notably in his book *Perestroika and New Thinking*, a personal credo which was lamentably short of a single fresh thought about nationalities policy. Contenting himself with spending a derisory five pages (out of 269) on 'The Union of Socialist Nations – A Unique Formation', Gorbachev conceded the desirability of greater mutual respect between nationalities but, in jargon worthy of Brezhnev, sententiously concluded that '*Soviet* patriotism' would ensure that 'we will still further strengthen the Union and Brotherhood of free peoples in a free country' (Gorbachev, 1988: 118–22).

Gorbachev's 'extraordinary complacency about, and insensitivity to, the "nationalities question"' moderated only slowly and grudgingly (Walker, 1993: 167). It was not until as late as February 1988 that he publicly changed his tune, coolly informing the CPSU central committee that the national question represented 'the most fundamental, vital question of our society'. Even after 1988, he still rested content with day-to-day crisis management as the momentum of the nationalist upsurge mounted: golden opportunities for major policy initiatives were repeatedly squandered (Hosking, 1991). Gorbachev did next to nothing before 1990 without the saving grace of doing it well. Often tactless, always patronising towards Russia's 'little brothers' within the Soviet 'Family of Nations', Gorbachev needlessly antagonised the more ambitious of the union republics (Nahaylo and Swoboda, 1990). Ambiguous and even contradictory signals were sent to the nationalities, leaving them bemused and eventually disillusioned. Gorbachev was generally not just reactive towards events but sluggish in that reaction, fostering the universal conviction that Soviet concessions could be extracted only under the duress of orchestrated nationality pressure (Walker, 1993). Where official strategy towards the Soviet nationalities was concerned, the accusation of stagnation which Gorbachev was so ready to level at the era of Brezhnev was just as appropriate to Gorbachev's own first five years of power.

Lest this interpretation reads like an indictment of Gorbachev, natural justice demands the consideration of a clutch of mitigating and countervailing factors influencing the Soviet leader. For example, Gorbachev's predilection for viewing the imperial issue in an economic rather than a national light misled him into a genuine undervaluation of its importance. Over the course of seventy years, virtually all regions of the Soviet Union had become so integrated into the centralised economic structure that the loss of any single component would inevitably both cripple the newly separated ex-component and skew the operation of the remaining components. Even the Baltic republics, which were the latest additions to the Soviet Union, had become near-indispensable to the Soviet economy over the last forty-five years. One of the most urgent arguments informing Gorbachev's refusal to decolonise the inner empire was that it was patently in no party's economic interest to do so (Remnick, 1994). Gorbachev was even to suggest that, in the remote eventuality of independence being sanctioned, the Soviet Union would demand a compensatory pre-payment for surrendering agricultural and industrial assets as a condition for the granting of independence. The idea of a conventional empire exacting financial compensation for the lost capital and income incurred by decolonisation is historically ludicrous. The very fact that such a recourse could be entertained in the Kremlin is another indication of the quite extraordinary character of the Soviet Empire.

Aside from the more predictable political and economic pressures to retain the inner empire, there remained a pervasive psychological dimension. At its most simplistic, many Russians had genuine difficulty understanding why non-Russians (and especially Ukrainians and Belorussians) should wish to become independent. Russian personalities as varied as Lenin, Sakharov and Gorbachev all underestimated the non-Russian preoccupation with independence, believing it to be merely an emotional response to past tsarist maltreatment. Once benevolent Soviet government was introduced, all non-Russians should speedily appreciate the proven material and ideological benefits of partnership (however junior) within a Russian-led state, and the appeal of separatist independence would evaporate. Like so many of his compatriots, Gorbachev could not 'grasp the visceral power of ethnic feeling' nor comprehend the often irrational appeal of nationalism to non-Russian nations, some of whom were prepared to reject Soviet preferential treatment and undergo considerable social and economic privation in the pursuit of independence (Stokes, 1993: 169).

Other explanations of Gorbachev's apparently dilatory treatment of the imperial issue centre upon his predicament as the 'captive in the Kremlin'. At the personal level, it is likely that Gorbachev's upbringing and circumstances led him to believe that the nationalist threat was less authoritative than it appeared. His career had not involved close or prolonged acquaintance with non-Russian nations, encouraging a politically disabling 'ethnic blindness' (Keep, 1995: 364). His own experience, mostly in the Stavropol area of the north Caucasus, was restricted to 'secondary nationalities' rather than 'primary nations', which may have disposed him to perceive all national groups as essentially deferential (or resigned) to Soviet authority, and therefore seriously to undervalue the aspirations of the union republics. A lawyer by training, Gorbachev may also have fallen victim to the occupational hazard of believing that legal niceties accurately reflected the realities of Soviet life, an astigmatic perception which the privileged lifestyle of a top *apparatchik* did little to correct (Walker, 1993). On various occasions, most famously on a Siberian walkabout in Krasnoyarsk in September 1988, Gorbachev was visibly shocked by the uncompromising smack of public

147

opinion, suggesting a sheltered existence which kept him ignorant of the practicalities of the Russian, let alone the non-Russian, everyday struggle for survival.

An ideological variant of the 'captive' explanation argues that Gorbachev had simply run out of options permissible within the framework of Soviet socialism. Over the seven decades of Soviet power, a succession of strategies had attempted unsuccessfully to square the stubborn resilience of national consciousness with a socialist ideology which declared nationalism a redundant anachronism. Leninist principles like 'National in Form, Socialist in Content', Stalinist slogans like the 'Friendship of Nations', Krushchevist buzz-words like *sblizhenie* (drawing-together) and *sliyanie* (fusion), and Brezhnevist concepts of the 'Soviet nation' and 'Soviet patriotism' all ended up in the capacious dustbin of Soviet history. Gorbachev casually binned the *sliyanie* doctrine in January 1989, unblushingly admitting that it was at very least unrealistic and probably morally wrong (Nahaylo and Swoboda, 1990). With all the stratagems consistent with Soviet Communism exhausted before his accession to power, Gorbachev found only non-socialist options remaining. His reluctance to adopt these options, thereby conceding the inability of Communism to solve the national question, accounts for his failure to take imaginative action until the Soviet 'flawed melting-pot' not only refused to melt but began to boil over (Hosking, 1991: 82).

As Gorbachev was forced into a fundamental rethink of the Soviet Union from spring 1990, the nationalist upsurge assumed unstoppable proportions. Although Lithuania was pressured into a temporary suspension of its proclaimed independence, the grudging promulgation of a Soviet secession law in April, establishing administratively unwieldy and politically inflammatory five-year procedures for the concession of independence for the union republics, proved a classic case of too little too late (Keep, 1995). Far from satisfying nationalist demands, the tantalising but arbitrarily deferred prospect of independence increased non-Russian agitation, as demonstrated most publicly and scandalously at the traditional May Day parade on Red Square in Moscow (Remnick, 1994).

The lead in what came to be called the 'Summer of Sovereignty' was assumed by Russia. In May 1990, the maverick Communist Boris Yeltsin, who had been sacked by Gorbachev as Moscow party boss in November 1987 for revealing too much about the *nomenklatura*'s privileged lifestyle, was elected President of the Russian Parliament. In June, the Russian Communist party followed the Lithuanian trend with a unilateral declaration of independence from the CPSU, pronouncing little less than a death sentence on the authority of the CPSU over the inner empire. In the same month, the Russian Parliament ruled that Russian laws took automatic precedence over Soviet laws within the Russian Federation, instituting a bitter 'War of Laws' which infected all other leading nations of the Soviet Union (Hosking, 1991; McAuley, 1992). Over the summer of 1990, all thirteen remaining union republics (since Lithuania already claimed to be independent) followed Russia in declaring their sovereignty. Although 'sovereignty' defined a moral right to self-determination (whether exercised or not), which was one stage short of a declaration of independence, the unanimity of the vote of no-confidence in the Soviet Union was politically devastating.

Russia's desertion of the Soviet banner astounded many Western observers but, given collapsing imperial will, it was not a complete surprise. While undoubtedly representing the 'imperial nation', Russians had never been necessarily the prime beneficiaries of Soviet rule, another feature which contradicts the conventional perception of empire. Under Soviet sway, the fastest economic and social progress had been registered in the central Asian republics, disposing the local population to prefer a campaign for greater autonomy over a drive for independence. Under Soviet rule, the highest standard of living had been enjoyed in the Baltic republics, a fact which irked the less well-off Russians and made the Baltic the favourite posting, migrant destination and retirement haven for Russians but did nothing to buy off the Estonians, Latvians and Lithuanians from their obsession with regaining independence.

At the level of intellectual counter-culture, the Soviet-exiled Alexander Solzhenitsyn had for a decade called for Russia to be permitted to play out her Slav destiny without unnecessary and debilitating colonial millstones. In his pamphlet *Rebuilding Russia*, published in September 1990, Solzhenitsyn proclaimed that 'the time has come for an uncompromising choice between an empire of which we ourselves are the primary victims and the physical and spiritual salvation of our own people' (Solzhenitsyn, 1991: 15). The most authoritative dissident Russian voice of the post-Stalinist Soviet Union was demanding that the inner empire be dismantled, shedding its parasitic colonies to allow a reconstituted Russia to pursue its proper mission free of imperial encumbrances (Remnick, 1994).

At the level of popular (and populist) national opinion released by *glasnost*, Russians were opting out of empire, believing that for too long they had been expected to foot the Soviet bill for the non-Russians' benefits and even extravagances. What bizarre kind of empire required the imperial nation to impoverish itself for the benefit of its greedy and manipulative colonies? What would seem preposterous in a conventional empire – the colonial periphery exploiting the imperial centre – now seemed intolerable in the Soviet Empire. As articulated by Yeltsin, the Russia-First declaration of summer 1990 developed by the end of the year into a separatist Russia-Only conviction which, even without the enthusiastic emulation of the non-Russian nations, represented 'a general constitutional crisis' and the supreme challenge to the integrity of the inner empire of the Soviet Union (Hosking, 1991: 155).

Moscow Meltdown

Entering 1991, Gorbachev worked tirelessly and not a little desperately to prevent the complete ruin of the Soviet Union, but the political odds against him were becoming mountainous. Deploring his accumulating presidential prerogatives, including the right to rule by decree from September 1990, Gorbachev's reformist allies were deserting him. Shevarnadze resigned as foreign minister in December 1990 in protest at impending dictatorship (Remnick, 1994). No longer (since February 1990) the automatic and privileged party of government, the CPSU was experiencing both nation-based schism and a collapse of *partiinost*. Many followed Yeltsin in resigning from the CPSU after its dispirited XXVIII Congress in July 1990. With three million members (or 14 per cent of total membership) quitting the party in 1990 alone, the CPSU was fast becoming a political shadow of its former omnipotent self (Walker, 1993: 156). At the same time, the very prospect of extinction drove the hardliners within the CPSU into reckless action: Soviet troops stormed the Vilnius TV tower in January 1991 as a warning to other union republics against either believing or emulating Lithuania's claim to independence (Keep, 1995).

Gorbachev's dogged efforts bore some fruit later in 1991. A first-ever referendum on the Soviet Union conducted in March was boycotted by Lithuania, Latvia, Estonia, Moldavia, Georgia and Armenia, the six smallest among the fifteen union republics, but registered the contradictory votes of 82 per cent supporting sovereignty and 73 per cent supporting the Union (Walker, 1993). Taking some heart from this admittedly dubious mandate, Gorbachev redoubled his efforts to salvage a necessarily altered but still recognisable Soviet Union. The only (if forlorn) hope was the speedy conversion of the sham federation inherited from Stalin into a genuine federation or confederation, justifiable as a return to the Leninist principles of the Constitution of 1924, by which nationally defined partners would join together without duress for mutual benefit.

The credibility of conversion was always problematic. Only as late as September 1989, on the eve of the decolonising of eastern Europe, had Gorbachev officially announced a 'renovation of Soviet federalism', a coincidence which left the nations of the Soviet Union cynical about the motives of the Soviet leadership. But in April 1991, the Novo-Ogarev or Nine-plus-One Accord was hammered out: the leaders of the nine union republics which had participated in the recent referendum pressured Gorbachev into conceding a shift towards a real Soviet federation in which all-Union functions were reduced to six closely defined areas of jurisdiction (Walker, 1993). By July 1991, against the background of the final dissolution of both Comecon and the Warsaw Pact, which set an irreversible seal on the decolonisation of the outer empire, Gorbachev finalised a new Union Treaty, which converted the inner empire of the Soviet Union into a territorially reduced but genuine federation of voluntary member states (Brown, 1991; Swain, 1993).

On 19 August 1991, the day before the new Union Treaty took legal effect, a *coup* was launched in the capital by a 'Gang of Eight', top-level Communist hardliners dismayed at what they regarded as the Soviet 'retreat to Muscovy'. In the Moscow street-theatre that ensued over the next two days, the hero of the hour was Boris Yeltsin. Having proved his personal popularity by a landslide victory in the elections to the presidency of Russia in June, Yeltsin seized the defence of the 'White House', the Russian Parliament building, as the supreme photo opportunity. With his political authority immeasurably boosted before both domestic and foreign audiences, Yeltsin was now determined to ban the CPSU and confiscate its physical and financial assets (Remnick, 1994; McAuley, 1992).

If Yeltsin was the principal beneficiary of the failed coup, it was Gorbachev who became its principal victim. Ignominiously confined to his holiday *dacha* in the Crimea as the crisis was played out, Gorbachev returned to Moscow to find himself in 'a different country' – effectively a de-Sovietised country – in which his political credibility was irreparably damaged. The total discrediting of the CPSU was symbolised by the rapturous toppling of the giant statue of Felix Dzerzhinsky, the founder of the Soviet secret police, outside the sinister Lubyanka jail in central Moscow on the night the *coup* failed. In a Yeltsin-orchestrated tableau of televised public humiliation, Gorbachev was forced to dismantle what remained of his political power-base by formally resigning as General Secretary of the disgraced CPSU and ordering the immediate dissolution of its Central Committee (Remnick, 1994: 494; Walker, 1993).

The botched neo-imperialist counter-revolution exploded Gorbachev's residual hopes for a revamped Soviet Union. All the republics signing the Nine-plus-One Accord were estranged from any manifestation of discredited Soviet authority, declaring their formal independence during late August 1991 (Keep, 1995). Through September and October, Gorbachev vainly mounted a damage limitation exercise: the transformed Soviet Union, pointedly renamed the 'Union of Sovereign States', would be a modest non-political entity strictly limited to 'the common economic space' (Walker, 1993: 186). But even the offer of this humblest possible form of survival could not dissuade any of the fifteen union republics from withdrawing their declarations of independence. Indeed in November, Yeltsin went further by announcing that in accordance with its full independence, Russia would now cease paying federal taxes to the All-Union Soviet government.

The final *coup de grâce* to the raddled Soviet Union was left to the Ukraine. The pivotal importance of the Ukraine as the key non-Russian republic for the future of any recognisable Soviet Union lay in its unique combination of demographic and economic weight. Although less than one-third as numerous as Russians, Ukrainians still comprised by far the second largest nation in the Soviet Union. Moreover, Ukrainians constituted over three-quarters of non-Russian Slavs, highlighting their contribution to the Slav Bloc and boosting their crucial importance to their Russian 'elder brothers' within the now-discredited Soviet 'Family of Nations'. Economically, an unhealthily high proportion of the total production of the Soviet Union – almost one-half of its agricultural products and over one-fifth of its industrial goods – was located in the Ukraine. To Gorbachev, the undisputable value of the Ukraine meant that its loss was the greatest single preventable disaster that could be visited upon the Soviet Union short of the apocalyptic defection of Russia. To Ukrainian nationalists, that same demographic and economic endowment was the clinching argument for the political independence of the Ukraine.

On 1 December 1991, the Ukraine held a full referendum to confirm or repudiate the government declaration of independence issued in late August: from an impressive 84 per cent turn-out, a massive 90.3 per cent voted for independence. In response to this unequivocal people-power mandate, the leaders of Russia, the Ukraine and Belorussia – Boris Yeltsin, Leonid Kravchuk and Stanislav Shushkevich – met near Brest-Litovsk on 8 December to issue the Belovezhskaya Pusha Declaration: the three Slav republics were seceding from the Soviet Union to form a Commonwealth of Independent States. 'This breathtaking piece of improvisation' was at first designed to be a select confederation of the three nations of the Slavic heartland of the defunct Soviet Union, but at a meeting in Alma Ata on 21 December, an invitation to join was extended to the other twelve union republics, eight of whom were to accept (Walker, 1993: 187). Stripped of all remaining illusions and recognising the unanimity of defection from anything even resembling the Soviet Union, Gorbachev resigned as President on Christmas Day 1991 (Keep, 1995). With no successor even considered, the rump of the Soviet Parliament acted with positively indecent haste to dissolve the Soviet Union. The once-proud red Soviet flag was rung down in the Kremlin the very next day.

The personal responsibility of Gorbachev for the revolution of 1989–91 has been debated ever since. Could the Soviet Union, for all its problems by the mid-1980s, have kept going without his ill-judged reforms and crass errors of judgement? To Soviet hardliners seeking a scapegoat for disaster, Gorbachev was an inept 'sorcerer's apprentice' dabbling in matters beyond his comprehension and ability, with predictably catastrophic results. (Brown, 1991: 5). Western commentators have been more inclined to play down the role of Gorbachev, claiming to discern an essentially pre-programmed, even inevitable sequence of events beyond the capability of any individual, however exalted, to influence (Keep, 1995: 415). Given the plight of the Soviet Empire, was Gorbachev on a hiding to nothing from as early as 1985? Belatedly aware that the prevailing odds were stacked against his *perestroika*, had Gorbachev no option but to go for broke from 1986? Like Dubcek in Czechoslovakia in 1968, Gorbachev was overtaken by the reformist 'Spring' which he both represented and released, progressively demoted into a doomed 'captive in the Kremlin' ever more transparently at the mercy of elemental forces beyond his control.

That the Soviet Union finally disappeared not only without a bang but with scarcely a whimper is testimony to the eventually unstoppable political and social transformation generated jointly (if not necessarily equally) by the 'impotence of the powerful' and the 'power of the powerless' throughout the Soviet Bloc from 1989. As in the outer empire of eastern Europe by 1989, so in the inner empire of the Soviet Union by 1991, the question of whether Communist jurisdiction constituted an 'empire' comparable with more traditional imperial phenomena became pedantically academic. To the overwhelming majority of the nations and nationalities of the Soviet Bloc (spectacularly not excluding the Russians themselves), the scenario of imperial twilight, an inevitable decolonisation and disintegration of the 'Last Empire', had become a universal commonplace. Just as 'Berlin 1989' overthrew the outer, eastern European Soviet Empire which was the legacy of 'Yalta 1945', so 'Moscow 1991' dissolved the inner, Eurasian empire of the Soviet Union bequeathed by 'Petrograd 1917'.

8

THE LAST EMPIRE?

Proverbially, the problem with life is that it must be lived forwards but can only be understood backwards. It is tempting to review the career of the Soviet Empire from the close but Olympian vantage point of the later 1990s and pontificate with all the glib self-confidence engendered by 20/20 hindsight. Aside from the inexcusable professional 'bad form' exhibited by indulgence in what E. P. Thompson once called 'the insufferable condescension of posterity', surrender to this temptation exposes the historian to (at least) three specific hazards. The first is the practical difficulty that the Soviet regime dedicated so many of its formidable resources to concealing the truth about itself that the level of involuntary ignorance of the dynamics of the Soviet Empire remains perilously high. The second is the historiographical likelihood that post-Soviet scholarship may at any time employ unprecedented access to hitherto confidential official documentation to revolutionise perceptions of the Soviet period. And the third is the political probability that developments within the ex-Soviet Empire during the late 1990s will colour retrospective historical interpretations of what may be termed the 'near-past'.

Without in any way underestimating the clear and present dangers of writing contemporary history, which are particularly valid with regard to the Soviet Empire, the politically high profile of a regime which ruled almost half the continent of Europe (and almost half of continental Asia) for nearly half the twentieth century renders a professional post-mortem on the Soviet body-politic historically imperative. While instantly conceding the provisional nature of the inquiry, the posing of a set of fundamental questions should facilitate a preliminary evaluation of the essential dynamic, overall career and historical significance of the Soviet Empire.

Designations and Definitions

First and most obviously, is 'empire' the most appropriate label to attach to the jurisdiction which prevailed over greater eastern Europe from 1945 to 1989/91? To suggest that the response depends on one's definition of 'empire' will be as disappointing as it is predictable for those seeking short and definitive answers. Without indulging in a lengthy disquisition on political semantics, it is apparent that the perception of what constitutes an 'empire' has changed considerably with the passage of time (Lichtheim, 1971). In the early modern era, *imperium* conventionally signified nothing more than a sovereign state. Later, 'empire' became a generalised term synonymous with first-division status: 'Muscovy' was officially rechristened the 'Russian Empire' in 1721 (following Peter the Great's territorial advance to the Baltic) to announce the presence of a new European 'Great Power'. By the nineteenth century, however, 'empire' across eastern Europe had come to suggest an amalgam of territories under dynastic leadership (as in the Habsburg and Ottoman Empires). In an era of mounting nationalism, 'empire' was increasingly perceived as at least a multi-ethnic and probably a multinational political entity 'dominated by persons of one nation over another nation' (Seton-Watson, 1961: 7).

Over the twentieth century, the pejorative connotations of 'empire' strengthened. After the First World War, the formal adoption of the nation-state as the moral building-block of the new international establishment inevitably cast 'empire', often vilified as 'a prison of nations', as the discredited (and hopefully discarded) manifestation of a pre-nationalist and pre-democratic past. After the Second World War, the headlong decolonisation of European empires in Africa and Asia was almost universally accompanied by an imperial guilt complex in the West which condemned 'empire' as both morally indefensible and politically bankrupt.

The Soviet Union could not conceive of itself as an 'empire', which constituted a uniquely capitalist power apparatus by which smaller and weaker territories were systematically exploited as subservient colonies for the exclusive benefit of the imperial establishment. By definition, Soviet jurisdiction, which was legitimised by socialism, could not constitute an empire. Consequently, Western descriptions of the Soviet Bloc after the Second World War as an 'empire' were as logically preposterous as they were politically outrageous. Moreover, the ongoing decolonisation of capitalist empires was creating a Third World which furnished an unprecedented opportunity for recruitment by Soviet-backed socialism. Far from being doomed to share the fate of the capitalist empires, the Soviet Bloc could expect to be the great beneficiary of decolonisation.

Post-1945 Soviet historiography even added a compulsory maritime element to its criteria for 'empire'. Although conceding that the nineteenth-century dynastic states of eastern Europe were commonly dubbed 'empires', the 'new empires' were western European-based bastions of advanced capitalism ruthlessly exploiting overseas colonies which had been opportunistically seized around the non-European world. This 'salt-water dimension' permitted the Soviet historical establishment to claim that not only the postwar Soviet Bloc and the interwar Soviet Union but even the pre-revolutionary tsarist state were not empires, since the historical expansion of their territorial jurisdiction had been dry-shod, exclusively across land. By employing the dual capitalist and maritime criteria, Soviet historiography disingenuously exculpated even tsarist but especially Soviet expansionism from the charge of imperialism.

The degree to which Soviet jurisdiction between 1945 and 1991 satisfied any or all of the extant definitions of 'empire' has generated something of an academic sub-discipline. To fall back on an anodyne dictionary definition like 'a multinational political entity' is conspicuously unhelpful, bracketing together constitutional federations (like Switzerland) with totalitarian dictatorships (like the Nazi *Neuordnung*). To carry a distinct and exclusive meaning, 'empire' must surely include as essentials the twin factors of systemic exploitation and involuntary membership (Seton-Watson, 1961). An inevitably unwieldy but reasonably precise definition of 'empire' might accordingly be 'a multinational sovereign state in which political, economic and social power is wielded by a readily identifiable élite for the purpose of the systematic exploitation of an involuntary membership of subordinated colonies and groups'.

By this rigorous (and perhaps loaded) definition, the Soviet Bloc may be broadly seen as an 'empire'. The distinction between exploiters and exploited was expressed in a geopolitical core-and-periphery pattern: within the Soviet Bloc, the 'People's Democracies' of eastern Europe were positioned around the Soviet Union in what may be called an 'Outer Empire'; within the Soviet Union itself, the fourteen non-Russian union republics comprised an 'Inner Empire' around the all-powerful Russian Republic. Throughout the career of this 'Empire', the political, strategic and economic exploitation of the colonial periphery by the imperial core was always the rule, most uninhibitedly in the late 1940s and early 1950s.

As a consequence, whatever the niceties of academic argument, the nations of eastern Europe perceived themselves as colonies of a Soviet Empire, involuntary inmates of a new 'prison of nations', a belief reinforced by the experiences of Hungary in 1956, Czechoslovakia in 1968 and Poland after 1980. Since 1989, the ex-colonies have insisted that their colonial experience was entirely negative, with no redeeming features or mitigating factors whatsoever. In reality, the exploitation was not always one-way: over the late 1950s and early 1960s, a number of colonies headed by Hungary secured preferential economic treatment which included regular and substantial subsidisation. Even so, the fact that the colonies could, on occasion, exploit the imperial power failed to impinge upon the east Europeans' conviction of their exclusive exploitation and demonstrates the un-usual and paradoxical nature of this 'Last Empire'.

If at least a *prima facie* case for inclusion within the genus of 'empire' has been established, what species distinct from the traditional dynastic empire and the new capitalist empire ruled eastern Europe over the later twentieth century? Various labels have been attached over the years, all arousing a measure of controversy, most possessing a degree of validity, none proving entirely satisfactory.

Ideological labels have always proved popular. 'Communist' suggests a primacy of ideological legitimation which the Soviet establishment might have been expected to approve; but objections came from both outside and inside the Soviet Bloc. Western commentators argued that genuine ideological commitment to communism had evaporated within the Soviet Union by the 1930s (at the very latest) and within Soviet eastern Europe by 1968 (at the very latest). Moreover, although the Bolsheviks officially added 'Communist' to the name of their party in 1918, they formally perceived communism as their ideological aspiration and eventual political goal. The gallows humour of eastern Europe responded to the orthodox slogan 'Communism is on the horizon' with the definition of 'horizon' as 'an imaginary line which retreats as you advance towards it and is consequently always the same immeasurable distance away'.

The generally preferred self-ascription of the establishment was 'socialist', a term which attempted to square ideological zeal with pragmatic modesty. Society had achieved miracles in reaching the stage of socialism but still had some distance to go before reaching the ultimate destination of communism. While expansion from the 'lesser empire' of the Soviet Union to the 'greater empire' of the Soviet Bloc could be portrayed as progress from 'Socialism in One Country' to 'Socialism in One Zone'; even Brezhnev at his most vainglorious never claimed to have progressed beyond 'developed socialism'. To the international socialist movement, however, the gravest reservations about the applicability of 'socialist' to what was happening first in the Soviet Union of the 1930s and then the eastern Europe of the late 1940s were harboured. Far from constructing the 'Bastion of Socialism', still less the 'Showpiece of Socialism', Stalin had instituted a discreditable regime which threatened to disgrace the embarrassed international socialist movement.

In the West, political labels have often been favoured over the ideological. Cynics have long argued that 'Russian' remains the most accurate descriptive adjective to attach to the 'Empire'. Despite the ideological gloss, which shifted from communism to socialism as its preferred legitimising rationale, the post-First World War Soviet Union and especially the post-Second World War Soviet Bloc were essentially power-systems designed and administered to ensure the primacy of Russian interests. In a famous speech in May 1945, Stalin claimed victory in the Second World War as an essentially Russian triumph: 'I propose a toast to the Russian people because it has earned in this war general recognition as the guiding force of the Soviet Union among all the peoples of our country' (Nahaylo and Swoboda, 1990: 95). For all the respect accorded the ideologically inspirational Bolshevik Revolution of 1917, the interwar 'lesser empire' and later the postwar 'greater empire' were fundamentally continuations of the fast-expanding nineteenth-century tsarist empire: the Soviet Bloc was 'the unsurprising empire... which reflected Russia's natural endowments for hegemony... [and had been] foreseeable for centuries' (Fernandez-Armesto, 1995: 187).

But while accepting that Stalin developed into something of a 'Red Tsar', there is a broader, symbolic significance in the fact that Josif Dzhugashvili could not, as a Georgian, be a 'Russian Tsar'. The Soviet regime undoubtedly placed the interests of Russia first among its strategic priorities; but its geopolitical size and demographic weight made the hegemony of Russia natural to the point of unavoidable. And although Russia was prioritised, Russians were not: the early Bolshevik party was embarrassing in its gross underrepresentation of Russians; the leadership contest of the late 1920s to succeed the part-Russian, part-German Lenin was between the Jewish Trotsky and the Georgian Stalin; and recruitment campaigns to bolster the new establishments in the 1920s and then the late 1940s favoured non-Russians over Russians to facilitate the stabilisation of a multinational empire. Though indisputably Russia-oriented, the Soviet personnel establishment outside the very highest organ of government, the fixedly Russian and Ukrainian-monopolised Politburo, was sufficiently multinational to refute the charge of an exclusively and selfishly 'Russian Empire' across post-1945 eastern Europe (Hosking, 1991).

'Stalinist' is a pejorative term tailored to the earlier, constructive period of empire, which was much favoured by Cold Warriors in the West. Certainly, the Stalinist system of authoritarian state power created in the Soviet Union over the 1930s was then employed to erect an empire out of the Red Army's occupation of eastern Europe during the late 1940s. But is it appropriate to attach the 'Stalinist' label to an imperial regime which lasted (just) into the 1990s when its architect died as early as 1953? While the fundamentals of Stalinist practice may have persisted through the four decades after Stalin's death, weathering sporadic de-Stalinisation campaigns, to dub the entire period 1945 to 1991 as 'Stalinist' unduly exaggerates the importance of the admittedly critical initial eight-year phase and minimises unacceptably the significance of authoritative imperial developments over the almost forty years which followed.

Despairing of precise or consensual ideological or political designations, some commentators have taken refuge in vaguer populist terms. 'Red' is a descriptive epithet attractive for neatly combining photogenic colour symbolism with echoing part-ideological, part-historical resonances. The red flag has represented popular radical commitment to socialism from the mid-nineteenth century, and became identified with the militant 'Guards' of 1917 and the Bolshevik-led forces in the civil war against the 'Whites' over 1918–21. And yet, 'Red' was too intimately associated with the earlier, heroic 'era of the barricades' to fit comfortably in the monochrome Stalinist era of totalitarian state control: even the all-conquering Red Army underwent official etiolation at the instant of its greatest triumph in 1945 to become the colourless 'Soviet Army'.

A discussion of alternative descriptive epithets to accompany 'Empire' invariably ends with the most obvious: 'Soviet'. As the preferred self-ascription of the Bolshevik state after 1922–4, 'Soviet' has commanded general international observance ever since. Strictly speaking, the term can be applied only to the jurisdiction of the Soviet Union itself, automatically excluding the parts of eastern Europe acquired during and after the Second World War and therefore disqualifying itself as an overall description of the entire bloc. Even so, as with 'Stalinist', the term 'Soviet' conveys the sense of a system created in the Soviet Union of the 1930s being imposed, typically by force and with minimal adaptation to local circumstances, upon eastern Europe after 1945. If the 'lesser empire' of the 1930s was indeed 'Soviet', the new eastern European territories of the 'greater empire' were 'sovietised' from the late 1940s onwards. Politically unambiguous but sufficiently anodyne to cover both 'Greater Russia' and 'Eastern Europe' for the entire period 1945 to 1991, 'Soviet' makes a convincing claim to be the least unsatisfactory of the terms available.

Rising and Falling

Having addressed, if not necessarily resolved, the essential but tiresome issue of nomenclature, it is high time to proceed to a consideration of the career of the designated 'Soviet Empire'.

When and why did the Soviet Empire rise? Patently, the empire in eastern Europe was created for a complex of military, strategic, economic, political and even ideological reasons emerging out of the Second World War. It can be cogently argued, however, that what happened over the 1940s was less the rise of a new empire than the expansion of an existing empire (Dalziel, 1993). The Soviet Union had existed as a 'lesser Soviet Empire' since the early 1920s, administering a smaller jurisdiction than the tsarist empire which it replaced but still constituting the largest and most multinational state in the world. From the late 1930s, the lesser Soviet Empire underwent a traumatic process of

164

territorial ebb and flow: first, expansion into eastern Europe during 1939–41; then expulsion from eastern Europe and much of European Russia from 1941–2; next, the recovery of its pre-1939 territory and 1939–41 acquisitions during 1943–4; and finally, the occupation of much of eastern Europe over 1944–5. A 'greater Soviet Empire' was created through the 'Sovietisation' of newly acquired territory, imposing the model of the early Stalinist period of the Soviet Union of the 1930s upon eastern Europe over the late Stalinist period of the 1940s (Seton-Watson, 1961). The process was accomplished through locally varying degrees of forcible imposition by the occupying Red Army (with the highest intervention in Poland, Hungary and Romania) and voluntary collaboration by the indigenous populations (with the greatest complicity in Czechoslovakia and, on the periphery of Stalinist authority, Yugoslavia and Albania).

But the Soviet Empire had *two* progenitors: the pre-war Soviet Union and the wartime Nazi *Neuordnung*. Over 1939–45, the German Empire self-interestedly liquidated many of the indigenous political cadres of eastern Europe, inadvertently clearing away the opposition for its imperial successor. By the irony of history, the New Order unwittingly did much of the Soviet Empire's dirty work for it, creating a power vacuum which the damaged and beleaguered Soviet Union found impossible to resist over the later 1940s. In effect, though not by design, the wartime Nazi 'New Order' facilitated a postwar Soviet 'Newer Order'. Given its parentage, it comes as no surprise that the Soviet Empire was seen by many hostile contemporaries as a 'Soviet *Ordnung*' or 'Stalinist *Reich*', inheriting the genetic characteristics of both forebears (Nahaylo and Swoboda, 1990: 97).

The concept of the phenomenal rise of the Soviet Empire is therefore an oversimplification of a complex train of events. The crucial decade of the 1940s witnessed not the sudden precipitation of a brand-new Soviet Empire but the development of a Greater Soviet Empire which represented both an expansion of the pre-war Soviet Union and an extension of the wartime *Neuordnung*. In that the emergence of the Soviet Empire was less cataclysmic and more organic than conventionally represented, its creation was less an event than a process, more a 'rising' than a 'rise'.

The phrase 'rise and fall' can also be misleading by its suggestion that the Soviet Empire was either rising or falling: the end of the rise was immediately followed by the start of the fall. In reality, the Soviet Empire experienced a protracted middle phase of 'neither rise nor fall' which ran broadly from the mid-1950s to the mid-1970s.

How should the middle period of the Soviet Empire be characterised? The Empire plainly enjoyed no heyday, no imperial glory days of uninhibited exploitation, supreme self-assurance and triumphalist swagger. Instead, a grimly defensive siege mentality pervaded the Cold War Empire: like the fabled Narnia imagined by C. S. Lewis, the Soviet Empire remained a joyless land where it was always winter but never Christmas. Nor did the Empire experience a prime, an era of safe consensus and comfortable stability. Imperial crises, which were regular to the point of rhythmic, ensured that no sooner was a stratagem adopted than it was subjected to strain. About every twelve years – in 1956, 1968, 1980 and 1991 – a fresh challenge from a different quarter of the Empire forced a tactical rethink and the adoption of a new line of policy from a dwindling list of available options. In the unsettling expectation of fresh and repeated challenge, the Soviet imperial establishment could never relax.

Even so, following the metaphor of rise and fall, the Empire did experience what may be termed a political plateau in mid-career, a period of fundamental security. From the mid-1950s to the mid-1970s, the Soviet establishment projected an aura of armour-clad permanence which was reinforced rather than contradicted by the imperial crises of 1956 and 1968, which gathered early momentum as local responses to campaigns of modest de-Stalinisation initiated by the Kremlin. Both the Hungarian and Czechoslovak crises demonstrated that, first, local eastern European forces could not successfully resist the imperial intervention of the Warsaw Pact to restore the Kremlin-determined geopolitical *status quo*; and secondly, that the West was prepared only to condemn Soviet repression and applaud east European resistance, not to take action other than (for shame) admitting a few political refugees. With insufficient resources of their own for effective defiance and only tokenistic support from the West, the conscripted eastern European nations were twice sharply reminded of the inefficacy of challenging imperial authority. Highlighted by the Berlin crisis of 1960–1 and the Cuban missile crisis of 1962, the global Cold War context of superpower confrontation injected a sense of the dogged maintenance of the external security and internal subordination of the Soviet Empire.

How did the Soviet Empire come to an end? Just as the Empire's 'rising' is better viewed as a process rather than an event, so with its 'falling'. The word 'fall' itself suggests a sudden and unforeseen calamity but a close analysis of the protracted Soviet ordeal would suggest that a two-phase 'decline and fall' is a more apt designation for the last fifteen years of the Empire.

From the mid-1970s to the mid-1980s, the Soviet Empire experienced a slow but accelerating decline. The 'normalisation' of eastern Europe imposed after 1968 deprived the Empire of its remaining shreds of ideological legitimacy, leaving a moral vacuum modestly but progressively exploited by religion, nationalism and the intelligentsia. Under Brezhnev's leadership, government degenerated into mere administration, a state of decay or stagnation (*zastoi*) in which pressing issues were shelved rather than addressed. By 1980, most of eastern Europe was on the verge of financial bankruptcy through massive indebtedness to the West. During the early 1980s, the Old Stalinist gerontocracy finally succumbed, some thirty years after the death of their professional benefactor and political inspiration, drawing a new generation into the highest offices of the Soviet state.

The completion of the fall is conventionally dated as autumn 1989 for eastern Europe and autumn 1991 for the Soviet Union. The beginning of the fall has been variously identified as the appointment of Mikhail Gorbachev to supreme Soviet power in 1985 and the turning-point year of 1987, when both *perestroika* and *glasnost* developed a momentum beyond the power of authority to halt, control or even channel. A complex interaction of overthrow from below – the people-power first identified by Vaclav Havel in his essay on 'The Power of the Powerless' – and collapse from above – the impotence of the powerful – effected the *annus mirabilis* of 1989 across the outer empire of eastern Europe. That same deadly combination of predominantly nationalist push-out and imperial pull-out spread east to contaminate the inner empire of the Soviet Union during 1990–1. On Boxing Day 1991, the Soviet Empire in all its former manifestations and past jurisdictions disappeared.

The overall shape to the life-history of the Soviet Bloc may now be seen as featuring, to retain past topographical imagery, four distinct phases: a sharply rising escarpment (from 1944 to the early 1950s); an undulating upland plateau (from the mid-1950s to the mid-1970s); a gradual but steepening downward slope (from the late 1970s to the mid-1980s); and a sudden and precipitous descent (from the late 1980s into the early 1990s). The changing gradients of political fortunes provided the Soviet Empire with a career profile whose silhouette was less a peak than a plateau, not so much a Matterhorn as a Table Mountain.

Weaknesses and Strengths

Why was the career of the Soviet Empire so brief? The sixty years of the lesser empire of the Soviet Union and the barely forty years of the greater empire of the Soviet Bloc make this imperial manifestation strikingly short-lived by comparison with other, more traditional empires. What accounts for the Soviet Bloc's apparent lack of imperial stamina?

A first explanation must be that the empire was over-extended from the outset. What has been called 'imperial overstretch' was forced upon Stalin by the exigencies of the Second World War (Kennedy, 1988). The material and human damage inflicted upon the European Soviet Union in 1941–4 was so devastating that Stalin had no option but to rely on the Asiatic Soviet Union more heavily than ever before and to retain and exploit newly acquired eastern Europe. The expansion of the pre-war Soviet Union into the postwar Soviet Bloc was not the venture of an ambitious empire confident in its mission but the almost panicky recourse of a defensive empire all too aware of its vulnerability. The descent of the Iron Curtain, interpreted by Western contemporaries as a demonstration of strength, appears in hindsight as an admission of weakness. Despite the increasingly questionable value of these colonial acquisitions, the surrender of such trophies of triumph in war was thereafter regarded as incompatible with the international prestige and *amour propre* of the Soviet superpower. The long-term effect of war-promoted and damage-induced territorial expansion was an over-extended super-empire which had mounting difficulties addressing the burgeoning peacetime demands of the Cold War era.

Among domestic demands, nationalism represented the greatest single challenge and the most persistent rival authority to the Soviet establishment. Though contained and managed by Soviet power, nationalism was never fully tamed or domesticated. Despite official confidence that nationalism's false dawn would be outshone by the high noon of socialism, the reality of national consciousness acknowledged in the pseudo-federalism of the Leninist Constitution in the 1920s was further recognised in the geopolitical structure of Yalta Europe in the 1940s. It may be tempting to follow the conventional line of perceiving the Soviet Bloc as a Cold War Empire freezing solid all overt opposition and unlicensed political alternatives; but although imposing an unwelcome chill-factor across its political micro-climate, the Soviet Ice Age gradually succumbed to global warming. In retrospect, it may seem that Soviet rule crisped up rather than froze national consciousness: the Soviet Empire proved less the deep-freeze than the dew-bin of eastern European nationalism.

A third reason for the relatively short career of the Soviet Empire is the unrelieved stress imposed by the Cold War. The experience of major war has been crucial to political developments in eastern Europe throughout the twentieth century: the

First World War bankrupted tsarism, offering the Bolsheviks an unexpected opportunity to seize power; the Civil War moulded the character of the Bolshevik state and determined the jurisdiction of the lesser empire of the Soviet Union; the Second World War forced expansion into the greater empire of the Soviet Bloc; and the Cold War first consolidated but ultimately debilitated the Soviet Empire to the point of total collapse. Like the dynastic empires in the First World War, the Soviet Empire performed too well militarily for its own good in the Cold War, eventually capitulating to the cumulative economic, social and political strains of the intolerably prolonged hostilities.

The semi-permanent strategic and military confrontation of the Cold War exacted enormous investment and expenditure, with new tests of superpower status – like the atomic arms race after 1945 and the space race after 1957 – remorselessly piling on the pressure to perform, whatever the domestic cost. Accorded superpower status prematurely in the late 1940s, the Soviet Union came under irresistible pressure to validate its false superpower reputation by expanding its economic reach into the Third World from the mid-1950s and claiming a global military reach by the early 1970s. Always something of 'a military giant but an economic dwarf', the Soviet Union became a hapless prisoner of its own propaganda, gradually impoverished and exhausted by its attempts to realise its grandiose superpower pretensions. The Soviet Union was condemned to suffer more than America over the long Cold War of attrition. The domestic cost was proportionately stratospheric for the Soviet Empire, whose military budget of at least 20 per cent of state expenditure contrasted starkly with the American level of a mere 4 per cent. Eventually, as America upped the power stakes over the 1980s, the top-heavy Soviet military superstructure could no longer be supported by a neglected economic and social infrastructure. By 1985, the Soviet Union could not sustain the roles of both warfare state and welfare state; by 1990, financial bankruptcy ensured that the stricken Soviet Union could sustain neither role.

A final explanation for failure lies in the more generalised observation that the Soviet Empire was an anachronism in the later twentieth century. The fact that the Soviet Bloc was apparently bucking the global trend towards accelerating, even galloping decolonisation of empire (especially in its 'plateau period' from the mid-1950s to the mid-1970s) persuaded some Western commentators of the inappropriateness of the term 'Soviet Empire'. And yet it is difficult to resist the all-too-familiar gibe about a Russian time-warp: throughout the modern period, Russia (in its various political manifestations) has been developmentally a century or more behind the West, desperately but ultimately unavailingly attempting to close the inherited gap through authoritarian state intervention. At its most tragifarcical, the 'Russia syndrome' ensures that Russia reaches a Western stage or achieves a Western standard just as the West moves on to the next stage or standard, rendering a frustrated and vulnerable Russia always one tantalising stage behind and adrift. By this explanation, the Soviet Empire was almost a political 'Land that Time Forgot', a naturally isolated (and then artificially insulated) haven for intimidating but doomed dinosaurs marooned outside the global mainstream.

A persistent critic might also argue that, as the delayed and therefore most anachronistic imperial phenomenon, the Soviet Empire was condemned to an unprecedentedly abbreviated career: in an era of ambient decolonisation, the Soviet Bloc was always living on borrowed time. The cycle of rise and fall which took most conventional empires centuries was accomplished by the Soviet Empire in mere decades. By a bitter irony, only in the pace of its imperial career was the Soviet Empire faster moving than the West. Trotsky had hoped that socialism might overcome inherited Russian backwardness through a 'telescoped revolution' in the Soviet Union; but history instead delivered a telescoped empire in the Soviet Bloc.

The question falling fast on the heels of 'why so short?' is inevitably 'then why so long?' If the Soviet Empire was as defensive, disadvantaged, overstretched and anachronistic as has been suggested, how did it manage to eke out its existence for as long as it did?

The most obvious explanation rests, in line with Mao Tsetung's aphorism that 'power grows out of the barrel of a gun', with the deployment of military force. Maintained by the Cold War Empire close to a 'hot war footing', the Soviet Army enjoyed a manpower and firepower on a scale justified by its reputation as the conqueror of the *Wehrmacht*. The Warsaw Pact became after its foundation in 1955 an increasingly integrated mechanism, which ensured that military force to maintain the *status quo* was always available to the Soviet Empire throughout its eastern European domains. Formidable enough to intimidate would-be opposition into sullen submission for most of the time, the Soviet Army and Warsaw Pact were, when required, effective if initially blunt instruments of repression: although the go-stop-go suppression of the Budapest Uprising by the Soviet Army in October–November 1956 exhibited glaring military shortcomings, the Warsaw Pact termination of the Prague Spring in August 1968 was skilfully executed in operational terms, a surgical-style intervention achieving its immediate objective with maximum despatch and minimum bloodshed. Despite the unsettling experience of the 'Soviet Vietnam' in Afghanistan after 1979, the Soviet Army (and other Warsaw Pact forces) retained its institutional morale, organisational cohesion and, above all, political reliability throughout the period from 1945 to 1991.

But it would be a mistake to presume that the Soviet Empire depended entirely on the 'stick factor': the undeniable importance of the 'permanent garrison' explanation cannot obscure the validity of the complementary 'carrot factor'. After the suffering of the Second World War and the privations of the late 1940s, living standards experienced a rapid and demonstrable improvement. By comparison with the low base of the 1940s, the material quality of life for the average citizen improved at almost spectacular rates throughout the plateau period of the mid-1950s to mid-1970s, sponsored first by Soviet subsidisation and later by Western investment. Only in the early 1980s did impending imperial bankruptcy effect an absolute decline in general living standards, prompting a popular double discontent during the late 1980s as the runaway media revolution permitted invidious comparisons with living standards in the West. That the Soviet

Empire failed to deliver the promised goods to ordinary citizens over its last decade destroyed its 'economic legitimation' and made an authoritative contribution to the people-power of the 1980s (Schopflin, 1993: 164). For most of its career, however, the Soviet Empire delivered a steadily improving material situation which undercut social and political opposition even within restive eastern Europe.

Another underrated factor maintaining the Soviet Empire was the flexibility of its imperial tactics. Imperial crises were countered by not only rapid-response military action but also dramatic switches of (especially economic) policy towards eastern Europe. The year 1956 prompted an economic volte-face, a switch from general and systematic extortion of eastern Europe to selective subsidisation of eastern Europe. 1968 prompted the abandonment of subsidisation in favour of a Soviet disengagement from eastern Europe. 1980 prompted selective re-intervention by Soviet authority to attempt to construct a financial rescue package for bankrupt eastern Europe. The wisdom or otherwise of Soviet imperial policies is certainly debatable; but the Soviet Empire was more supple and responsive to crises than has generally been recognised, undermining the conventional caricature of a dinosaur too sclerotic and lethargic to adapt to changing circumstances. At the same time, it is undoubtedly true that Soviet pragmatism operated only within strict parameters: since the maintenance of the Soviet Empire was non-negotiable until 1989 itself, tactical flexibility was at least matched by strategic inflexibility.

A final contributory explanation for the Empire's relative longevity lies with its relationship with the West. It has become a commonplace to suggest that the Soviet Empire was finally bankrupted by the USA raising the stakes of the Cold War to breaking-point for the Soviet Union, a simplistic but not entirely unfounded interpretation. But if the West precipitated the final crisis of the Soviet Empire in the 1980s, it had also perpetuated the declining Soviet Empire over the 1970s. As the Soviet Union economically disengaged from its colonial periphery after 1968, the financial spectre which now stalked eastern Europe was exorcised by investment from the West. In effect, near-bankrupt eastern Europe was bailed out by the West in the 1970s, post-poning the supreme financial crisis of the Soviet Empire through external 'subsidisation'. By accident or design, Western economic intervention in eastern Europe offered the Soviet Empire a financial reprieve and deferred the Soviet supreme crisis by a decade, even though it also ensured that when that inevitable crisis finally came, it would be apocalyptic. Without this suppor-tive Western investment in eastern Europe, the moribund Soviet Empire would have moved from decline to fall in the late 1970s rather than the late 1980s.

Vices and Virtues

With the cataclysmic two-stage collapse of the Soviet Empire during 1989–91 still fresh in the minds of spectators and participants, it is naturally the deficiencies of the Empire which have attracted most attention. The incontrovertible fact of the Empire's demise is simultaneously irrefutable testi-mony to (at the very least) its political failure and lack of long-term viability. Whether in terms of shortcomings, misdemea-nours or crimes, just what was so reprehensible about the Soviet Empire?

A cardinal shortcoming was the Empire's inefficient and wasteful economic performance. Although the Stalinist com-mand economy was not without its achievements (at a price) in targeting the industrial challenges of the 1930s and 1940s, it became glaringly mismatched to the increasingly sophisticated economic needs of the Empire from the 1950s. Khrushchev's bold attempts to modernise through institutional de-Stalinisation and the licensing of a mixed socialist-capitalist economy were regarded as 'too much too early' by the Stalinist bureaucracy, which atavistically dumped such 'creeping capitalism' after 1968. During the period of stagnancy in the 1970s, the Brezhnev establishment was able to keep going through fortuitous good luck rather than even tolerably good management. By the time that Gorbachev revived Khrushchevite ideas on the desirability

174

and practicability of a mixed economy in the late 1980s, a doomed atmosphere of 'too little too late' hung over the commitment to *perestroika*. By its last decade, the sprawling, outdated and dysfunctional economy of the Soviet Empire could neither deliver the welfare state by fulfilling the economic and social expectations of its population nor supply the warfare state by satisfying the rocketing financial and technological demands of the Cold War.

Just when the Soviet system suffered ideological (as distinct from economic) bankruptcy is a question which has taxed Western historians for some time. Some critics of communism would date Bolshevism's crisis of faith as early as 1921, when Lenin insisted on the tactical abandonment of War Communism in favour of the semi-capitalist New Economic Policy. Many others would cite the 1930s, when the Second Revolution of Stalin put a survival premium on obedience to authority over allegiance to ideology. Still more would see the Nazi–Soviet Pact of 1939 as a body-blow to the ideological credibility of the Soviet Union within the global socialist movement. While ideological commitment by indigenous populations played a larger role in the 'communist takeover' of eastern Europe in the 1940s than has usually been represented, the ordeal of subordination to the Soviet Empire soon disappointed the majority. Although portrayed by some as a straight contest between socialism and nationalism, '1956' further spelled out the primacy of power politics within the Empire. Soon '1968' effectively completed the process of ideological disillusionment: if even the reformist Czechoslovak initiative was punished as too radical a divergence from the obligatory Soviet model, then Soviet totalitarianism had triumphed (Stokes, 1993). Thereafter, ideological commitment was reserved for the opposition to a Soviet Empire which was universally perceived as based upon naked self-interest rather than anything more than cynical lip-service to the official slogans of Marxism–Leninism.

In the course of the career of the Soviet Empire, its society became increasingly, and eventually insufferably, divisive and atrophied. In the teeth of Communist claims of social egalitarianism, the great divide between the rulers and the ruled became more hermetic than in many states in the capitalist West. During the 1940s, the ousting of the upper- and middle-class enemies offered exceptional (and, as it turned out, unrepeatable) opportunities for the upward social mobility of the lower classes across eastern Europe. Once safely ensconced in political power, however, the new personnel establishment of the Soviet Empire was determined to retain, safeguard and bequeath to the next generation its social privileges by preventing subsequent upward social mobility (Hosking, 1985). The recently promoted lower-class establishments of the Stalinist era were broadly retained as ageing establishments up until the 1980s, with only the occasional purge to threaten their self-perpetuating inter-generational ascendancy. The breakthrough generations of the 1930s in the Soviet Union and the 1940s in the Soviet Empire, the beneficiaries of Stalinism, devoted themselves to guarding and perpetuating for the rest of their lives the system from which they had so brazenly benefited. From the 1950s, upward social mobility became exceptional, the rule of patronage and inheritance became the rule. By the 1970s, the Stalinist-created establishment was socially exclusive and politically stagnant. Only the inexorable march of time finally removed the atrophied geriatric establishment of Stalinist dinosaurs over the 1980s.

Still further up the scale from 'shortcomings' to 'crimes' is the political repression which was so characteristic of the Soviet Empire. The Cold War Empire exacted both a war economy and a war society. Over the Stalinist late 1940s, ideological alternatives to communism were ruthlessly eliminated and oppositional parties were first excluded from power and then suppressed through the operation of the all-powerful state security services. Formerly sovereign nations were forcibly debased into Soviet POWs within a new 'prison of nations'. The culture of authoritarianism was maintained with only minor fluctuations, modest concessions and relative diminution throughout the career of the Soviet Empire. The civil and human rights of the populace of the Soviet Empire were systematically violated in the interests of the authoritarian state.

Moreover, repression dominated both the ruled and the rulers. Having established a power-monopoly through the liquidation of all opposition, the new Communist establishments of eastern Europe were themselves purged to ensure optimum 'discipline', that is to say absolute and unconditional subordination to Kremlin authority. Although a measure of autonomy was permitted to the east European colonies from the 1950s, any major threat to imperial authority brought prompt military intervention and punitive political purges of the offending local establishment. Throughout its career, the principal motif of the Soviet Empire was the systematic, if scrupulously differentiated, terrorisation of rulers and ruled alike.

Although naked political repression tended to decrease, economic inefficiency actually increased, and ideological bankruptcy and social atrophy were gradually effected over the period from the late 1940s to the late 1980s, cumulatively amounting to a damning indictment of the sins of commission and the sins of omission of the 'Evil Empire' of the Soviet Bloc.

Is there nothing to be said in defence of the Soviet Empire? In the immediate aftermath of imperial collapse, it was, of course, wildly unfashionable to suggest that the Soviet Empire registered any achievements whatsoever. Conventionally, newly independent ex-colonies are disposed to look back on their colonial experience as an exploited and benighted condition from which no benefits could possibly accrue. But the challenges confronting the 'Soviet successor states' in the 1990s have already prompted a selective nostalgia for the Soviet past which reinforces the need for historians to attempt an interim reassessment of the overall record of the Soviet Bloc. Without proposing anything as fundamental as retrospective rehabilitation, a clutch of benefits of the Soviet Empire may still be tentatively identified.

The first achievement was a welfare state which established basic minimum living standards in the aftermath of the Second World War. The undisguisable shortcomings of the Soviet welfare system were part of the common currency of Cold War propaganda, particularly in the 1980s when an absolute decline in standards was spotlighted by growing awareness (through *glasnost*) of 'relative deprivation' in comparison with the West. Certainly, the provision of housing, medical care and social welfare for the ordinary citizen was sub-standard by comparison with the West throughout the period 1945 to 1991. But the feat of providing replacement accommodation and establishing an empire-wide welfare system across Soviet jurisdiction over only a decade following the ruinous Second World War has been unsung or underestimated. Over the plateau period from the mid-1950s to mid-1970s, universal literacy was broadly achieved, unemployment disappeared (even if jobs had to be invented to soak up the available labour force), and consumer goods like washing-machines and especially TVs (admittedly with poor specifications and performance) appeared in ordinary homes. To sneer at Soviet failure to perform a miracle – to match Western standards of consumer provision – is to fail to appreciate the degree of Soviet recovery from the devastation of the Second World War.

Like many more traditional empires of the past, the Soviet Empire also provided many of the advantages of a large politico-economic entity. Smaller nations naturally dwell upon their ignominious colonial status, the frustration of their national aspirations and their exploitation for the exclusive benefit of the imperial establishment. Ex-Soviet nations have been reluctant to admit the existence of any benefits accruing from involuntary membership of the large-scale, multinational Soviet polity. And yet centralised authority within the Empire featured positive as well as the more obvious negative aspects. Modern communications, though never reaching Western specifications, were extended and integrated throughout the imperial jurisdiction. Whether by constitutional fiat (like Article IV of the Comecon Charter of 1960) or through standardised bureaucratic procedure, Russian quickly became the *lingua franca* of the Soviet Empire: though often resisted by patriotic non-Russians, the *lingua russica* served as the integrative common denominator of day-to-day communication.

Available imperial financing was on a scale far beyond the reach of individual component colonies. Sometimes, notably

over the first decade of the Empire, the colonies were compelled
to contribute more to the imperial treasury than they received,
suffering a net loss. More often, notably over the late 1950s and
early 1960s, the colonies contributed less than they received by
way of imperial investment or subsidisation, making a handsome
net profit. The financial profit-or-loss equation demonstrably
varied from period to period and from state to state within
eastern Europe, but with the overall trend showing a decrease
in the negative features and an increase in the positive features
for the Soviet colonies as a whole over the entire imperial era
from 1945 to 1989/1991.

A third achievement of the Soviet Empire was its damping-
down of nationalist squabbling throughout eastern Europe. The
nationalism inherent in the interwar lesser empire of the Soviet
Union was subjugated by a combination of expedient constitutional recognition of national identity and ruthless executive
repression of non-Russian activism. The nationalism which had
unsettled 'Versailles Eastern Europe' was similarly neutralised in
the postwar greater empire by a combination of tacit recognition
of the interwar geopolitical *status quo* and merciless subordination
of the eastern European colonies to the imperial priorities of the
Soviet Bloc. Although (as already suggested) nationalism was
never really domesticated, still less rendered redundant by the
appeal of socialism, it was effectively kennelled for most of the
period 1945 to 1989/1991. Even the classic imperial crises of
1956, 1968 and 1980 onwards, all of which featured nationalist
motivation to varying degrees, were not simply and exclusively
nationalist rebellions against a Soviet 'prison of nations'. During
the Soviet period, the nationalism of the colonies was regarded
by the liberal, de-colonising West as an emancipatory force to be
applauded. In the post-Soviet period, the nationalism of the ex-
colonies has exhibited unsavoury integral and irredentist characteristics which have left many Western observers with real (if
guilty and unadmitted) respect for the social policing and political stabilisation imposed by the *pax sovietica*.

Still on the subject of peace (or at least order), the Soviet
Empire contributed to an almost unprecedentedly long period

of international stability. Although both the Soviet Union and the United States indulged in proxy wars over the years 1945 to 1991, such interventions were strictly confined to conventional warfare within the Third World. Direct superpower conflict was avoided throughout. Even the episode which brought the nuclear apocalypse closest – the Cuban missile crisis of 1962 – had the effect of bringing down Khrushchev, the creator of confrontation, and reinforcing the implicit Cold War *status quo*. Up until the early 1980s, the longer the Cold War went on, the more phoney it became, geared to last indefinitely in order to justify bloated military establishments within both the Soviet Union and the United States and to legitimise superpower spheres of influence rather than to precipitate Armageddon. In this respect, the permanent partition of Europe which Stalin sought from Hitler in 1939 but which lasted only eighteen months was realised on a grander scale in the Cold War partition which lasted almost forty-five years.

Although justified as an unavoidable fight to the death between the crusading, mutually exclusive universalist ideologies of communism and capitalism, the Cold War developed into a self-interested superpower charade, a cosy condominium for which both the Soviet Union and the United States were prepared to settle. The Soviet Empire was already so overextended that although the opportunistic planting of colonial outposts was occasionally indulged, no serious commitment to major expansion was ever undertaken. The postwar Soviet Bloc had every intention of maintaining international (as well as internal) peace and stability for the foreseeable future, to the long-term benefit of Europe, East and West.

Like most conventional empires, the Soviet Empire had beneficiaries as well as victims and displayed a mixed historical record of not only weaknesses and vices but strengths and virtues, which defies absolute judgements and easy generalisations. After the denunciations which accompanied decolonisation, the West has come to recognise the ambiguities in its own imperial performance but has barely started to acknowledge the manifest ambivalences in the case history of the Soviet Empire.

Falling and Rising

Responding belatedly to the provocative title of this final chapter, our concluding question must be whether the late Soviet Empire was really the 'last empire'. The distinction between 'late' and 'last' is revealing: the Soviet Empire is 'late' both in the sense of being recently deceased and chronologically challenged by comparison with other past empires; but whether it turns out to be the 'last', either globally or within the traditional Eurasian context, is a speculative talking-point as fascinating for a world community on the brink of the twenty-first century as it is dangerous for a contemporary historian tempted into prophecy.

It would certainly seem that within the geopolitical zone which was for almost half a century the undisputed power-jurisdiction of the Soviet Empire, the accelerating process of withdrawal, decomposition and dissolution has run its full course: the outer empire of eastern Europe was decolonised over autumn 1989 and the inner empire of the non-Russian Soviet Union disappeared over autumn 1991. But the fall of the Soviet Empire was not completed by the termination of the Soviet Union in December 1991. The next two years were characterised by a disintegrative era of free fall, in which the minor non-Russian nationalities secured considerable autonomy for themselves within what may be regarded as the 'innermost empire' of the Russian Federation.

Since 1993, however, runaway disintegration has bottomed out and evidence of determined Russian territorial reintegration has been unmistakable. Although Russian President Boris Yeltsin has called the ongoing war against Chechnya since December 1994 his 'greatest mistake', there was no statesmanlike alternative to his firm line in this test-case for nationality secessionism within the Russian Federation.

Over the same period, an atmosphere of imperial afterglow has been transformed into a climate of imperial *revanche*. Dismissed at the time of its creation in December 1991 as a political fig-leaf to conceal the naked embarrassment of the collapse of the Soviet Union, the Commonwealth of Independent States (CIS) has become, at very least, a Russian-led economic-based confederation of rapidly expanding membership. The circumstances in which Georgia was constrained to join the CIS in March 1994 and Belarus relinquished most of its independence within a 'Commonwealth of Sovereign Republics' in April 1996 warn of a Russian neo-imperialist campaign to recover at least some of the territory of the defunct Soviet Empire. The non-Russian periphery of the ex-Soviet Union has increasingly been regarded as 'near-abroad', a natural and legitimate sphere of strategic, military and economic influence for Russia. The near-triumph of the populist nationalist Vladimir Zhirinovsky in the Russian elections of December 1993 demonstrated a widespread outrage at the humiliation of Russia, a mood of open defiance of the West and a blustering threat to go on the territorial rampage. In the event of a real or imagined Western infiltration of the 'near-abroad', Russia may be tempted to establish a mini-empire covering most of the jurisdiction of the former Soviet Union.

Having witnessed the rise and fall of the Soviet Empire from the mid-1940s to the early 1990s, will the later 1990s see the fall and rise of a new Soviet Empire? It seems certain that although empire may well strike back, it will not be Soviet. Although the cadres of the Soviet Empire have adjusted with egregious dexterity to the triumph of capitalism, as evidenced by the electoral successes of 'retread Communist' parties across East–Central Europe during 1993–4, the ideology of communism has been irremediably discredited. Even the State Duma's condemnation of the abolition of the Soviet Union in March 1996 and the strong showing of the Russian Communist leader Gennady Zyuganov in the presidential elections of June–July 1996 cannot be represented as mass ideological re-dedication.

The geopolitical shape of the future eastern Europe is still in a process of crystallisation which may take what remains of the twentieth century to complete, but an imperial comeback of a non-Soviet character cannot be ruled out. It would seem likely that the 'far-abroad' of East–Central Europe which secured its independence in 1989 will be safe from Russian *revanche* through voluntary and ever-closer association with the EU. By contrast, the 'near-abroad' of most of the non-Russian republics of the former Soviet Union already incorporated into the CIS may well be consolidated into a Russian-controlled neo-empire within a Yalta-II Europe. A Russian 'successor state' to the Soviet Union may no longer be a superpower in a confrontational Cold War; but Russia fully intends to be a Great Power in the competitive 'War of the Soviet Succession'.

To suggest that the Soviet Bloc constituted the 'last empire' has an unconvincing overarching philosophical finality associated with the end of history argument. Empire has found so many ideological justifications even within the limited compass of the twentieth century, ranging from dynasticism through socialism to nationalism, that it is tempting to view empire as an essentially supra-ideological phenomenon. Ideologies may come and go but empire is historically more resilient, a power-system which tailors its legitimising ideology pragmatically and often cynically to the demands of political exigency. To attempt to maintain even a socialist-justified but over-extended late Soviet Empire in an era of imperial decolonisation may indeed have proved anachronistic; but the Soviet Empire may well turn out to be the latest rather than the last manifestation of imperialism. To consign the phenomenon of empire, whether globally or within its favourite habitat of greater eastern Europe, to the dustbin of history would surely be both presumptuous and premature.

BIBLIOGRAPHY

Ascherson, Neal, *The Polish August* (London, 1981).

Auty, Phyllis, *Tito* (London, 1974).

Bethell, Nicholas, *Gomulka* (London, 1972).

Brogan, Patrick, *Eastern Europe 1939–1989: The Fifty Years War* (London, 1990).

Brown, Archie, *The Gorbachev Factor* (Oxford, 1996)..

Brown, J. F., *Eastern Europe and Communist Rule* (Durham, N.C., 1988).

Brown, J. F., *Surge To Freedom: The End of Communist Rule in Eastern Europe* (Durham, N. C., 1991).

Brzezinski, Zbigniew, *The Soviet Bloc: Unity and Conflict* (Cambridge, Mass., 1966).

Brzezinski, Zbigniew, *The Grand Failure* (New York, 1990).

Carrere d'Encausse, Helene, *Decline of an Empire* (New York, 1979).

Carrere d'Encausse, Helene, *Big Brother: The Soviet Union and Soviet Europe* (New York, 1987).

Charlton, Michael, *The Eagle and the Small Birds: Crisis in the Soviet Empire: from Yalta to Solidarity* (London, 1984).

Crampton, Richard, *Eastern Europe in the Twentieth Century* (London, 1994).

Crankshaw, Edward, *Putting Up with the Russians, 1947–1984* (London, 1984).

Cullen, Robert, *Twilight of Empire: Inside the Crumbling Soviet Bloc* (London, 1991).

Dalziel, Stephen, *The Rise and Fall of the Soviet Empire* (London, 1993).

Djilas, Milovan, *The New Class: An Analysis of the Communist System* (London, 1957).

Dubcek, Alexander, *Hope Dies Last: The Autobiography of Alexander Dubcek* (New York, 1993).

Dunbabin, J. P. D., *The Cold War: The Great Powers and their Allies* (London, 1994).

East, Roger, *Revolutions in Eastern Europe* (London, 1992).

Feher, Ferenc and Heller, Agnes, *Hungary 1956 Revisited* (London, 1983).

Fejto, François, *A History of the People's Democracies* (London, 1974).

Fernandez-Armesto, Felipe, *The Times Illustrated History of Europe* (London, 1995).

Fukuyama, Francis, 'The End of History?', *The National Interest*, vol. 16 (1989).

Garton Ash, Timothy, *The Polish Revolution: Solidarity 1980–1982* (London, 1983).

Garton Ash, Timothy, *The Uses of Adversity: Essays on the Fate of Eastern Europe* (New York, 1989).

Garton Ash, Timothy, *We, The People: The Revolution of 1989* (Harmondsworth, 1990).

Glenny, Misha, *The Rebirth of History: Eastern Europe in the Age of Democracy* (Harmondsworth, 1990).

Gorbachev, Mikhail, *Perestroika and New Thinking* (Moscow, 1988).

Havel, Vaclav, *The Power of the Powerless* (New York, 1985).

Hosking, Geoffrey, *A History of the Soviet Union* (London, 1985).

Hosking, Geoffrey, *The Awakening of the Soviet Union* (London, 1991).

Ionescu, Ghita, *The Breakup of the Soviet Empire in Eastern Europe* (Harmondsworth, 1965).

Kaldor, Mary, *The Imaginary War: Understanding the East–West Conflict* (Oxford, 1990).

Keep, John L. H., *Last of the Empires: A History of the Soviet Union, 1945–1991* (Oxford, 1995).

Kennedy, Paul, *The Rise and Fall of the Great Powers* (London, 1988).

Khrushchev, Nikita, *Khrushchev Remembers* (London, 1971 and 1974).

Lafeber, Walter, *America, Russia and the Cold War* (New York, 1967).

Lichtheim, George, *Imperialism* (London, 1971).

Mason, David S., *Revolution in East–Central Europe: The Rise and Fall of Communism and the Cold War* (Boulder, Col., 1992).

Macartney, C. A. and Palmer, Alan, *Independent Eastern Europe* (New York, 1962).

McAuley, Mary, *Soviet Politics 1917–1991* (Oxford, 1992).

McCauley, Martin, *The Soviet Union since 1917* (London, 1981).

Molnar, Miklos, *Budapest 1956* (London, 1971).

Mooney, Peter J., *The Soviet Superpower: The Soviet Union, 1945–80* (London, 1982).

Morris, L. P., *Eastern Europe since 1945* (London, 1984).

Murphy, Paul J., *Brezhnev: Soviet Politician* (Jefferson, N. C., 1981).

Nahaylo, Bogdan and Swoboda, Victor, *Soviet Disunion* (London, 1990).

Narkiewicz, Olga, *Eastern Europe, 1968–1984* (London, 1986).

Okey, Robin, *Eastern Europe, 1780–1985: Feudalism to Communism* (2nd edn., London, 1986).

Pearson, Raymond, *National Minorities in Eastern Europe 1848–1945* (London, 1983).

Pearson, Raymond, *European Nationalism 1789–1920* (London, 1994).

Polonsky, Antony, *The Little Dictators: The History of Eastern Europe since 1918* (London, 1975).

Ponton, Geoffrey, *The Soviet Era: From Lenin to Yeltsin* (Oxford, 1994).

Pravda, Alex, *The End of the Outer Empire: Soviet–East European Relations in Transition, 1985–1990* (London, 1992).

Pryce-Jones, David, *The War that Never Was: The Fall of the Soviet Empire, 1985–1991* (London, 1995).

Read, Piers Paul, *Ablaze: The Story of Chernobyl* (London, 1993).

Remnick, David, *Lenin's Tomb: The Last Days of the Soviet Empire* (London, 1994).

Rhodes James, Robert, *The Czechoslovak Crisis 1968* (London, 1969).

Roskin, Michael G., *The Rebirth of East Europe* (2nd edn, Englewood Cliffs, N. J., 1994).

Rothschild, Joseph, *Return to Diversity: A Political History of East Central Europe since World War II* (Oxford, 1989).

Rudolph, Richard L. and Good, David F. (eds), *Nationalism and Empire: The Habsburg Empire and the Soviet Union* (New York, 1992).

Rupnik, Jacques, *The Other Europe: The Rise and Fall of Communism in East–Central Europe* (London, 1988).

Sakwa, Richard, *Gorbachev and his Reforms* (London, 1990).

Schopflin, George, *Politics in Eastern Europe, 1945–1992* (Oxford, 1993).

Selbourne, David, *Death of the Dark Hero: Eastern Europe, 1987–1990* (London, 1990).

Seton-Watson, Hugh, *Eastern Europe between the Wars, 1918–1941* (Cambridge, 1945).

Seton-Watson, Hugh, *The East European Revolutions* (London, 1956).

Seton-Watson, Hugh, *The New Imperialism* (London, 1961).

Shawcross, William, *Dubcek* (London, 1970).

Simons, Thomas W., *Eastern Europe in the Postwar World* (2nd edn, London, 1993).

Solzhenitsyn, Alexander, *The Gulag Archipelago* (London, 1974 and 1975).

Solzhenitsyn, Alexander, *Rebuilding Russia* (London, 1991).

Stokes, Gale (ed.), *From Stalinism to Pluralism: A Documentary History of Eastern Europe since 1945* (Oxford, 1991).

Stokes, Gale, *The Walls Came Tumbling Down: The Collapse of Communism in Eastern Europe* (Oxford, 1993).

Swain, Geoffrey and Nigel, *Eastern Europe since 1945* (London, 1993).

Sword, Keith (ed.), *The Times Guide to Eastern Europe* (London, 1991).

Tampke, Jurgen, *The People's Republics of Eastern Europe* (London, 1983).

Taylor, A. J. P., *The Origins of the Second World War* (London, 1961).

Tismaneanu, Vladimir, *Reinventing Politics: Eastern Europe from Stalin to Havel* (New York, 1992).

Tolstoy, Nikolai, *Stalin's Secret War* (London, 1981).

Tomaszewski, Jerzy, *The Socialist Regimes of East Central Europe: Their Establishment and Consolidation, 1944–67* (London, 1989).

Ulam, Adam B., *The Communists: The Story of Power and Lost Illusions, 1948–1991* (New York, 1992).

Walesa, Lech, *The Struggle and the Triumph: An Autobiography* (New York, 1992).

Walker, Martin, *The Cold War* (London, 1994).

Walker, Rachel, *Six Years that Shook the World: Perestroika, the Impossible Project* (Manchester, 1993).

White, Stephen, *Gorbachev and After* (Cambridge, 1991).

Windsor, Philip and Roberts, Adam, *Czechoslovakia 1968: Reform, Repression and Resistance* (London, 1969).

Wright, Martin, *Soviet Union: The Challenge of Change* (London, 1989).

Yeltsin, Boris, *Against the Grain: An Autobiography* (London, 1990).

Young, John W., *Cold War Europe, 1945–1989* (London, 1991).

Zeman, Z. A. B., *Prague Spring* (London, 1969).

Zeman, Z. A. B., *The Making and Breaking of Communist Europe* (Oxford, 1991).

INDEX

Index

superpowers 29–30, 42, 60, 61, 103–4, 110, 111, 116, 167, 170, 180, 183
Svoboda, Ludvik 77
Szklawska Poreba 33

Teheran Conference 22, 23, 25
televorot (TV revolution) 91, 115–16, 123, 133, 140, 152
thaw 45, 48, 66, 112
Third World 52, 84–5, 93, 115, 159, 170, 180
Tiananmen Square massacre 127, 128, 131, 144
Tito, Josip 34–6, 38, 43, 46, 51, 105
Titoism 36, 37, 43, 51, 52, 53, 80
Togliatti, Palmiro 46
Tokes, Laszlo 132
Trotsky, Leon 6, 8, 9, 39, 66, 162, 171
Truman, Harry 25, 31
Truman Doctrine 30
Tsarist Empire 2, 3, 4, 6, 7, 8, 10, 16, 20, 57, 142, 147, 159, 162, 164, 170
Two Camp Doctrine 49

Ukraine 6, 7, 19–21, 41, 50, 82, 117, 119, 122, 139–40, 143, 147, 153–4, 163
Ulbricht, Walter 48, 76
Union of Sovereign States 153
Union Treaty 144, 151–2
United Kingdom 13, 14, 15, 18, 22, 24
United Nations 70, 128
United States of America 10, 13, 14, 22, 25, 27, 29–33, 42, 57, 60, 61, 68–70, 74, 86–7, 92, 93, 99, 102, 103–4, 106, 110, 111–12, 170, 173, 180

Vaculik, Ludvik 78
velvet revolution 132
Versailles Europe 10–15, 17, 18, 19, 22, 24, 26, 30, 31, 179
Vietnam 87, 100, 102–3, 116, 172
Vilnius 137, 151
Vysotsky, Vladimir 91

Walesa, Lech 97, 125
War Communism 67, 175
Warsaw 16, 23, 78, 97, 98
Warsaw Pact 50–1, 58, 74, 77–8, 85–6, 97, 98, 100, 128, 129, 132, 152, 166, 172
Wehrmacht 16–21, 26–7, 172
Wilson, Woodrow 10
Winter War 18–19

Yalta Conference 22–5, 30, 155
Yalta Europe 1, 45, 55, 63–4, 87, 123, 125, 133, 169, 183
Yeltsin, Boris 149–54, 181
Yevtushenko, Yevgenii 67
Yugoslavia 11, 13, 16, 19, 20, 21, 27, 34–6, 40, 43, 45, 51–2, 53, 55, 56, 77, 105, 143, 165

zastoi (stagnation) 89, 90–1, 105, 110, 112, 117, 146
Zhdanov, Andrei 47, 49
Zhivkov, Todor 131
Zhulin, Alexei 67
Zyuganov, Gennady 182